Turning Teaching into Learning:
The Role of Student Responsibility in the Collegiate Experience

by Todd M. Davis and Patricia Hillman Murrell

ASHE-ERIC Higher Education Report No. 8, 1993

Prepared by

Clearinghouse on Higher Education
The George Washington University

In cooperation with

Association for the Study
of Higher Education

Published by

School of Education and Human Development
The George Washington University

Jonathan D. Fife, Series Editor

Cite as

Davis, Todd M., and Patricia Hillman Murrell. 1993. *Turning Teaching into Learning: The Role of Student Responsibility in the Collegiate Experience.* ASHE-ERIC Higher Education Report No. 8. Washington, D.C.: The George Washington University, School of Education and Human Development.

Library of Congress Catalog Card Number 94-67645
ISSN 0884-0040
ISBN 1-878380-29-X

Managing Editor: Bryan Hollister
Manuscript Editor: Alexandra Rockey
Cover design by Michael David Brown, Rockville, Maryland

The ERIC Clearinghouse on Higher Education invites individuals to submit proposals for writing monographs for the *ASHE-ERIC Higher Education Report* series. Proposals must include:
1. A detailed manuscript proposal of not more than five pages.
2. A chapter-by-chapter outline.
3. A 75-word summary to be used by several review committees for the initial screening and rating of each proposal.
4. A vita and a writing sample.

ERIC Clearinghouse on Higher Education
School of Education and Human Development
The George Washington University
One Dupont Circle, Suite 630
Washington, DC 20036-1183

This publication was prepared partially with funding from the Office of Educational Research and Improvement, U.S. Department of Education, under contract no. ED RR-93-0200. The opinions expressed in this report do not necessarily reflect the positions or policies of OERI or the Department.

EXECUTIVE SUMMARY

Recent scholarship has emphasized the importance of student effort and involvement in their academic and cocurricular activities as the decisive elements in promoting positive college outcomes. As colleges have struggled to extend opportunities, an accompanying expectation for students to assume responsibility for their own education often has been lacking. Institutions must work to create a climate in which all students feel welcome and able to fully participate. It is equally important to nurture an ethic that demands student commitment and promotes student responsibility. Students can contribute to their own learning and to the development of a campus climate in which all can grow and learn.

What Is Student Responsibility?
Colleges are learning communities, and individuals accepted into these communities have the privileges and responsibilities of membership. If we are to communicate our expectations, we must offer a set of standards and examples that moves our discussion from generality to practice. Robert Pace has offered such a set of standards and has embedded them in the College Student Experience Questionnaire (CSEQ).

The CSEQ is based on the proposition that all learning and development requires an investment of time and effort by the student. At the heart of the CSEQ is a set of scales which defines the dimensions of student responsibility. These scales are called "Quality of Effort" scales in that they assess the degree to which students are extending themselves in their college activities. The domains include the use of classrooms, libraries, residence halls, student unions, athletic facilities, laboratories, and studios and galleries. The social dimension is reflected in scales that tap contacts with faculty, informal student friendships, clubs and organizations, and student conversations. Pace's work gives the academic community a map of the terrain of student responsibility and suggests concrete activities that contribute directly to student growth and learning.

Why Is Student Responsibility Important?
First, student responsibility is the key to all development and learning. Research has demonstrated that college outcomes are tied to the effort that students put into their work and the degree to which they are involved with their studies and campus life. Second, irresponsible students diminish our collective academic life. Within an individual classroom, the

behavior of even a few highly irresponsible students or, worse, a large number of passive, disaffected students can drag a class down to its lowest common denominator. For an institution, the erosion of an academic ethos can lead to a culture that is stagnant, divisive, and anti-intellectual.

Third, the habits of responsible civic and personal life are sharpened and refined in college. Will employers, international economic competitors, or future history itself be tolerant of students who fail to develop sufficient self-control and initiative to study for tests or participate in academic life? Finally, if colleges are to reclaim the public trust, they must learn not to make promises that cannot be kept. Colleges have responsibilities to students and society. Yet, colleges are not *solely* responsible for the outcomes of their students. A clear acknowledgment of the mutual obligations of all members of the academic community is a prerequisite to restoring the academy's balance and clarity of purpose.

What Are the Foundations of Student Responsibility?

Professors Pace, Tinto, Pascarella, and Astin have offered explicit theories about how colleges can promote student learning and growth. Despite different uses of terms, these approaches have much in common. First, each theorist recognizes that the student's background plays a role in shaping college outcomes. This role is largely indirect and is moderated by the college environment and a student's interactions with faculty and peers. Second, each theorist sees the campus environment exerting an enabling effect on college outcomes. Last, all emphasize the importance of a partnership between the college and the student. Colleges alone cannot "produce" student learning. Colleges provide opportunities for interaction and involvement and establish a climate conducive to responsible participation. Each approach reflects the centrality of what we call student responsibility.

The body of research derived from the work of these theorists represents one of the strongest and most sustained accounts of what it takes to succeed in college. The review indicates that the effects of initial group differences on college outcomes are relatively slight and largely mediated by the manner in which the student engages the college experience. Generally, college students appear more alike than different. The college context has two elements: 1) the structural features of the organization and 2) the climate or "ethos."

Structural features that tend to isolate students and promote an ethos of anonymity produce poor college outcomes. College climates characterized by a strong sense of direction and which build student involvement tend to promote favorable outcomes by promoting student-faculty and student-peer relations, as well as establishing an expectation that students will behave responsibly. Finally, the decisive single factor in affecting college outcomes is the degree to which students are integrated into the life of the campus, interact with faculty and peers, and are involved in their studies.

How Can We Encourage Responsible Student Behavior?

Institutional policies and practices must be oriented toward developing a climate in which students' responsibility and active participation in their own collegiate experience are promoted. Policies that stress the importance of student achievement and in-class and cocurricular challenge and support are essential for student growth. The institutional culture clearly must convey the institution's purpose in an unambiguous manner, and the ethos of the campus must be one in which students believe they are members of a larger community. As student culture serves as a filter for students entering college, care must be taken to ensure that students who are prepared inadequately understand the nature of college life and what is expected to attain satisfactory academic and developmental gains.

Small-scale, human environments must be built in which students and faculty collectively can engage in the process of teaching and learning. As learning is the process through which development occurs, it is crucial for students to be actively engaged in the classroom. Course activities are the vehicle through which students may become more fully engaged with academic material. The literature clearly indicates that the quality of effort that a student expends in interactions with peers and faculty is the single most important determinate in college outcomes.

This report concludes with a call for a new relationship between our institutions of higher learning and our students. A genuine shared purpose among all members of the higher education community can be created by recoupling individual rights with a sense of personal and social responsibility around issues of teaching and learning. The work of Pace is a good place at which to begin thinking about the renewal of our intellectual community. As Pace reminds us, all learning is the mutual responsibility of students, faculty, and administrators. Student responsibility doesn't just happen. We must expect it, foster it, and nurture it.

ADVISORY BOARD

Barbara E. Brittingham
University of Rhode Island

Jay L. Chronister
University of Virginia

Rodolfo Z. Garcia
Michigan State University

Elizabeth M. Hawthorne
University of Toledo

Bruce Anthony Jones
University of Pittsburgh

L. Jackson Newell
University of Utah

Carolyn Thompson
State University of New York–Buffalo

CONSULTING EDITORS

J. Kent Caruthers
MGT of America, Inc.

Elsa Kircher Cole
The University of Michigan

Jane F. Earley
Mankato State University

Walter H. Gmelch
Washington State University

James O. Hammons
University of Arkansas

Robert M. Hendrickson
The Pennsylvania State University

George D. Kuh
Indiana University–Bloomington

Barbara A. Lee
Rutgers University

Yvonna S. Lincoln
Texas A&M University

Frances Lucas-Tauchar
Emory University

Kathleen Manning
The University of Vermont

Robert J. Menges
Northwestern University

Leila Moore
The Pennsylvania State University

Amaury Nora
University of Illinois–Chicago

Robert M. O'Neil
University of Virginia

C. Robert Pace
University of California–Los Angeles

Raymond V. Padilla
Arizona State University

Scott Rickard
Association of College Unions–International

G. Jeremiah Ryan
Harford Community College

Frances Stage
Indiana University–Bloomington

Kala Stroop
Southeast Missouri State University

Ellen Switkes
University of California–Oakland

Jo Taylor
Wayne State University

Carolyn J. Thompson
State University of New York–Buffalo

Caroline Turner
University of Minnesota–Twin Cities

Elizabeth A. Williams
University of Massachuetts–Amherst

Richard A. Yanikoski
DePaul University

REVIEW PANEL

Kenneth C. Green
University of Southern California

Edward R. Hines
Illinois State University

Marsha W. Krotseng
West Virginia State College and University Systems

George D. Kuh
Indiana University–Bloomington

Daniel T. Layzell
University of Wisconsin System

Meredith Ludwig
American Association of State Colleges and Universities

Mantha V. Mehallis
Florida Atlantic University

Robert J. Menges
Northwestern University

Toby Milton
Essex Community College

James R. Mingle
State Higher Education Executive Officers

Gary Rhoades
University of Arizona

G. Jeremiah Ryan
Harford Community College

Mary Ann Sagaria
Ohio State University

Daryl G. Smith
Claremont Graduate School

William Tierney
The Pennsylvania State University

Susan Twombly
University of Kansas

Harold Wechsler
University of Rochester

Michael J. Worth
The George Washington University

CONTENTS

FOREWORD

During the past several years, the ASHE-ERIC Higher Education Report Series has published a number of reports focusing on teaching skills. *Active Learning: Creating Excitement in the Classroom* (Bonwell and Eison 1991) discusses how to increase teaching effectiveness and knowledge retention by actively involving students in such higher-order skills as analysis, synthesis, and evaluation. *Critical Thinking: Theory, Research, Practice, and Possibilities* (Kurfiss 1988) analyzes the three perspectives dominating the current literature on critical thinking: argumentative skills, cognitive processes, and intellectual development. *Learning Styles: Implications for Improving Educational Practices* (Claxton and Murrell 1987) examines how recognizing different learning styles based on personality, information processing, and social interaction can help instructors promote more effective learning. *Cooperative Learning: Increasing College Faculty Instructional Productivity* (Johnson, Johnson, and Smith 1991) reviews the results of higher achievement, more positive relationships, and healthier psychological adjustments that learning cooperatively produces in contrast to the more traditional model of individualistic experiences.

What is a common underlying theme in those publications—more specifically addressed in this report—is that the learning process is dependent on students taking responsibility for using the information they are presented. Under the more traditional mode of teaching—the lecture—faculty present an organized set of information and the students record it in a way in which they can relate it to other information. As one faculty member put it to a class, "My job is to talk and your job is to listen. Let's hope that we complete our jobs at the same time."

The lecture method is still the most popular form of teaching. Faculty like it for several reasons. First, it is the technique they have seen used most often by their own teachers, and therefore it is the easiest to model. Second, it gives faculty a sense of control—they know that students have had a chance to be exposed to a minimum body of important knowledge because the instructors personally have included the information in their lectures. And third, it gives the faculty members peace of mind, because they know that once the knowledge has been integrated into their lecture material, they have done their job and are no longer responsible for the learning outcome. If the results are poor, it is because "the student is not capable of doing the work." This method is passive in student involvement, reactive in learning responses, and, for the professor, free of responsibility for student learning outcomes.

What the recent research on student learning has concluded is that the more students are actively involved in the learning process and take personal responsibility for their learning outcomes, the greater are the learning results. This report, co-authored by Todd M. Davis, associate professor in the Higher Education Administration Program at the University of North Texas and director of research at the Institute of International Education in New York, and Patricia Hillman Murrell, director of the Center for the Study of Higher Education and professor in the Department of Leadership at the University of Memphis, examines the literature on student responsibility. Specific issues such as quality of effort, student background, and college environment all influence college outcomes. In the final section, the authors reflect on the implications of student responsibility for inquiry and practice.

The more individuals accept personal responsibility for the outcomes of their actions, the more likely they are to achieve those outcomes. The collegiate experience is one of nurturing and training. It is not expected that students automatically will possess certain skills; most of the time these skills must be developed. The better that faculty accept their responsibility to help instill in their students a sense of ownership in the learning process, the greater will be the long-term impact of the academic experiences of the students. This report will help to establish a rationale and procedures to ensure the success of this partnership of turning students into learners.

Jonathan D. Fife
Series Editor, Professor of Higher Education Administration, and Director, ERIC Clearinghouse on Higher Education

ACKNOWLEDGMENTS

As the reader soon will discover, a great deal has been written about student responsibility during the past 20 years. So much, indeed, that a professor's usual excuse to write a book—which is that there is no suitable text—is absolutely untenable. In considering the work of Astin, Pascarella, and Tinto and especially that of Robert Pace we were struck with the common themes that ran through the writings of these professors. We believe that the time has come to present a synthesis of this body of work which will speak to the single most compelling issue of our times. That issue centers around finding the balance between individual rights and the responsibilities that members of a community have to themselves and to each other.

As postmodern thinkers will tell us, there is no such thing as a value-free social science. Clearly this monograph reflects the intersection of our personal and professional autobiographies with the substantial body of literature that this slender volume spans. While our reading of the literature clearly is our own, we acknowledge our debt to the academics before us who labored in the vineyard so that we might now drink the wine.

Our debt to those colleagues who, in varied and tangible ways, advanced this project to final form is deep. We extend our thanks to Nancy Matthews and Lucy Williford, to Gopika Mehta, who tried to teach an old dog a set of new tricks, and to Dwane Kingery for a grant that helped defray the costs of the project.

To our spouses Jane Furr Davis and Dan S. Murrell, who both too often deferred their own projects during the writing of this monograph . . . for this we are most grateful.

Finally, TMD honors a special debt to Louis and Matilda, Milton, Hortense, Beatrice, Mortimer, Francis, and Leona, who already understand, and to Claire, Hamilton, Frances, and Elliot, who soon will know.

INTRODUCTION TO STUDENT RESPONSIBILITY

Everybody is obliged to be responsible.
Charles Dickens

*I believe that every right implies a responsibility; every oppor-
tunity an obligation; every possession, a duty.*
John D. Rockefeller Jr.

John strolled into class and expressed surprise when he
realized we were having a test. I reminded him that the test
date was on the syllabus. "Oh," John whined, "I lost the syllabus. Can I take a makeup next week?"

"I'm sick and tired of this apathy," says a professor as he
walks back to his office and slumps in a chair. "How do I
teach a seminar class when no one bothers to read any of the
assigned articles?"

"Students expect to be spoon-fed," moans a chemistry professor. "I spend the bulk of lab time explaining simple experimental procedures that they should have read themselves.
Then they get frustrated when they can't finish the experiment
on time."

*This state of
affairs
progressively
undermines
the most
fundamental
goals of an
academy.*

The stories are familiar. They have been told many times in
various versions in college halls and faculty offices around
the world: stories of students' lack of involvement with their
studies, stories that faculty tell of their frustration with students' failure to realize that learning in college does not come
about by merely showing up in class. Students only take from
their experiences what they put into them.
Incidents of student irresponsibility indeed are so common
that many in the academy, especially less-experienced faculty,
regard these situations as facts of academic life. In truth, the
vignettes reflect an ethical lapse that constitutes a serious barrier for individual students and for the intellectual life of the
academy. Whether due to the student's developmental stage,
lack of cultural preparedness, or even a societally sanctioned
celebration of indolence, these attitudes contribute to a cor-
rosive atmosphere in the classroom and on campus. This state
of affairs progressively undermines the most fundamental
goals of an academy: to nurture individual development, foster a sense of civic responsibility, and promote learning
among students. The challenges for collegiate educators are
to understand how institutional efforts interact with student

responsibility; to craft policy; and develop instructional responses which promote students' involvement in their education. A student's collegiate gains do not flow exclusively from institutional efforts. We must affirm the role of student accountability for their own academic progress and the importance of student responsibility to make the most of the college experience.

A college education in the United States is seen as the ticket to upward mobility and professional life. As our two-year and four-year colleges and universities extended this opportunity to all comers to live the American dream, they also faced an unprecedented challenge. The college experience no longer is the prerogative of traditional-aged, bright students. It now also encompasses nontraditional populations. Many of these first-generation college students are unaware of the expectations of college life or have significant extracurricular demands.

Clearly, it is necessary for an institution to create a climate in which all students, especially those new to the academy, feel welcome and able to fully participate. Beyond this, it is equally important to nurture an ethic that demands student commitment and promotes student responsibility. Students should be more than passive transients through an institution. They must become active, responsible, and empowered participants in their own learning and development.

As colleges have struggled to extend opportunities, an accompanying expectation for students to assume responsibility for their own education often has been lacking. Some have characterized the tendency for an institution to add services and lower expectations as contributing to a campuswide "culture of dependency" (Friedlander, Murrell, and McDougal 1993). In this climate, students expect institutions to do more and more, while their own responsibility for participation becomes less and less. By promoting an ethic of student responsibility as a crucial component in the relational experience of learning, institutions can work toward developing policies that promote a sense of obligation. Students, faculty, and college administrators also can contribute to the development of a campus climate in which all can grow and learn.

Defining Student Responsibility
Colleges are learning communities. Individuals who are accepted into these bodies have the rights and privileges of

membership. They also incur responsibilities. *Responsibility* is defined as a duty or obligation by the *American Heritage Dictionary*. The first definition of *responsible* is the ethical accountability of an individual for the care or welfare of others. The second definition involves personal accountability or the ability to act without superior guidance. While there is a legal dimension to the concept of responsibility, this report is concerned with the moral dimension. The examples of irresponsible student behavior cited at the beginning of this section remind us that the moral (obligatory) values of responsibility do not carry the sanctions of law. The obligations of a student are specific to the collegiate context.

The dictionary definition of responsibility implies that the obligations we incur as students are for self and others in our association. The concept of student responsibility is not a dry or lifeless topic: It is a concept that is central to the way we, as individuals and collectively, shape our lives. How we order our own lives is directly connected to our disordered public life.

Robert Bellah, in his provocative book *Habits of the Heart*, says,

> . . . *public life is built upon the practices of commitment that shape character. These practices establish a web of interconnection by creating trust, joining people to families, friends, communities, and churches, and making each other aware of his reliance on the larger society. They form those habits of the heart that are the matrix of a moral ecology, the connecting tissue of the body politic* (Bellah et al. 1985).

According to Bellah, we find ourselves only when we develop moral relationships with others and in the process contribute to the maintenance of a vital public life. The Association of American Colleges report of the Task Group on General Education suggests that the core programs of our colleges and universities must "consider the meaning and value of our common life and responsibility to each other as human beings."

Student responsibility is an essential ingredient for student development. A student who is open to the experiences that college offers is going to begin the process of reconstructing a world vision that is complex and based on inner-directed sensibilities rather than external authority. Ultimately, responsible involvement in college will promote the formation of habits that become the foundation for participation in civic life. This issue of responsibility has important implications well beyond an individual's college years. Our way of knowing—our epistemology—becomes our way of being, and habits developed in college have a way of showing up in later life (Palmer 1987). Thus, the development of an ethic of responsibility has powerful implications for the workplace and the larger community, where collaboration is valued and the common good is paramount. While we may agree on the importance of developing an ethic of student responsibility, there are difficulties applying this concept to the real world of college life.

There are two basic difficulties with our consideration and application of student responsibility: accountability and specificity. Let's first consider accountability. Accountability implies that individuals are responsible when their conduct fails to meet an accepted standard. Two synonyms for *responsible* are "answerable" and "accountable." When a moral obligation is incurred, one is answerable to some other authority. Failure to meet the expectation is subject to review and appropriate action; to be subject to such a review, an individual must be held accountable. But what exactly is the standard?

Thomas Lickona reminds us that responsibility and respect are the two great moral values that jointly constitute the basis for ethical life (1991). Respect emphasizes the proscriptive and points us toward the "thou shall not's" of life. Responsibility emphasizes the prescriptive: the "do unto others" and the "love thy neighbor" dimensions of ethical life.

In prescribing student behavior, we are able to be quite specific. The injunction that "students will not throw spitballs in class" is easily communicated and understood. Conversely, the call for students to participate in class doesn't tell the student whether we mean attending class, active note taking, keeping up with class reading, participating in class discussion, or all of the above and then some. Likewise, being prepared for class may entail bringing the appropriate materials, reviewing assigned readings and notes, studying with others, etc.

While some would say, "Why, it's obvious what 'being prepared for class means,'" we have difficulty delineating and communicating precisely what is meant by responsible student behavior. How, then, can a student be held accountable?

To what standard or set of standards is a student answerable? While a complete enumeration of responsible student behavior in all areas of collegiate life is not possible or even desirable, we can define the broad areas of student life in which responsible behavior is expected and provide a set of examples that will move our discussion from the realm of theory to the world of practice. In the next section we shall discuss the contributions of Robert Pace, who has done precisely this.

C. Robert Pace and Student Responsibility
Robert Pace is a man with common sense. He is one of the most respected and highly acclaimed scholars in the field of higher education and has focused his efforts on linking theory and practice. During the past 15 years, his principal energies have been directed toward the development and use of an instrument designed to assess the quality of effort that students put into their collegiate experience (Pace 1984, 1987, 1990). The College Student Experience Questionnaire (CSEQ) is rooted in the obvious proposition that all learning and development requires an investment of time and effort by the student. Pace is fond of pointing out that when students are asked if they agree with the statement, "If students expect to benefit from what this college or university has to offer, they have to take the initiative," more than 95 percent agree (Pace 1982).

While students recognize their role in the educational process, Pace argues that our colleges and governing boards have lost sight of this commonsense fact. As he plainly notes:

> *Much of the current rhetoric about institutional account-ability and consumerism in higher education is one-sided. If students don't graduate, the institution is accountable. If students don't learn, the teacher is accountable. If the graduates don't get good jobs, the institution is to blame* (1984, p. 6).

Learning in college is a joint proposition. Students are accountable—responsible for involving themselves in their class work, taking advantage of the opportunities and resources provided by the college and the faculty, and carrying their studies into their lives and relationships. Ultimately, students must transform their educational experiences by making these experiences part of their way of being and using what

they learn. Colleges are accountable, and so are faculty. They are accountable for providing first-rate resources and facilities. They are responsible for designing curriculum that is up-to-date and relevant. They are responsible for teaching students in a way that enables them to link their studies with their lives and for making instruction accessible to students.

The CSEQ is used by higher education institutions concerned about the mutual responsibility of students, faculty, and administrators in attaining college outcomes. As we will use the CSEQ to delineate areas of student responsibility, let us review some of its basics. At the heart of the CSEQ is a set of scales that describe important categories of college experiences. We take these categories to define important dimensions of student responsibility. The CSEQ provides a way to articulate the specific behaviors that are inherent in responsible student involvement in college life. It is particularly helpful because it sends a message to all interested campus constituencies that the college experience is a coherent whole that requires a facilitative climate and student effort. These scales are called "Quality of Effort" scales in that they assess the degree to which students are extending themselves in their college activities.

The content of the Quality of Effort scales is derived from two basic propositions. First, the scales, or content domains, tap the effort that students put into using the colleges' resources and facilities and the effort they expend in developing contacts in a variety of collegiate relationships. Pace believed that the most important factors in accounting for student growth were those found on the college campus, especially the physical and human resources and opportunities available on the campus. Thus, the areas in which students might expend effort would be those connected with campus facilities and interpersonal interactions. Second, the activities that are included in the scales are directly observable and based in behavior. By grounding the Quality of Effort scales in observables, students have an opportunity to objectively characterize their own behavior.

Of the 14 Quality of Effort scales, seven are concerned with use of facilities and seven with the investment of effort in personal and social relationships. The domains or scales include the use of classrooms, libraries, residence halls, student unions, athletic facilities, laboratories, and studios and galleries. The social dimension is reflected in scales which tap contacts with faculty, informal student friendships, clubs and organizations, and student conversations. The items that define each scale are expressed in behavioral terms, and students are asked to indicate how often they have engaged in a particular activity during the academic year by marking "never," "occasionally," "often," or "very often." Scale items are arranged in a sequence from those that reflect relatively modest or common forms of effort to those that require a considerable display of initiative. Appendix 1 presents the structure of the Quality of Effort scales in some detail. It may be useful to refer to this appendix at different points throughout this report to clarify the scope of the scales.

Student responsibility implies that students can be held accountable for the quality of their actions. The effort that students put forth in making the most of the opportunities available defines the extent to which they are behaving as responsible students. The 14 scales give the academic community a map of the moral terrain of student responsibility. The individual items provide concrete examples of the types of responsible use of facilities and social engagement that are essential for student growth and learning.

Why Is Student Responsibility Important?

There are some questions whose answers may initially seem obvious yet, upon reflection, have deeper implications. This is one of those questions. We have described the concept of student responsibility and have suggested its importance. There are four basic reasons why this topic must be addressed by those concerned with higher education.

First, student responsibility is the key to student development and learning. During the last 20 years, research on student outcomes has unambiguously demonstrated that college outcomes are tied to the effort that students put into their work and the degree to which they are involved in their studies and campus life. Can the virtue of responsibility be taught? Socrates said that it can only be taught by example. If we acknowledge this truth, then our colleges have an extended obligation to craft policies that actively promote student effort. Faculty have an obligation to teach in a manner that provides opportunities for students to involve themselves in their studies and extend that learning into their lives.

Second, irresponsible students diminish our collective academic life. Such students hurt themselves and other members of the academic community. A campus community depends on the active participation of all members. The irresponsible behavior of a few students can weaken the fabric that has brought students and faculty together. Within an individual classroom, the behavior of even a few highly irresponsible students or, worse, a large number of passive, disaffected students can drag a class down to its lowest common denominator. For an institution, the erosion of an academic ethos can lead to the development of a culture that is stagnant, divisive, and anti-intellectual.

Third, the habits of responsible civic and personal life are sharpened and refined in college. One of the goals of higher education in a democracy is to prepare students for participation in that democratic society. As membership in society confers both rights and responsibilities on its members, so must it be in a college society. If our colleges are to fulfill this important purpose, they must nurture a climate in which students are active participants in their college education. Will employers, international economic competitors, or future history itself be tolerant of students who fail to develop sufficient self-control and initiative to study for tests or participate in academic life?

Finally, student responsibility has implications for public policy toward higher education. If colleges are to reclaim the public trust, they must learn not to make promises that cannot be kept. Colleges have responsibilities to students and to society, yet colleges are not *solely* responsible for the outcomes of their students. If students are unwilling to do their part, then outcomes will be less than satisfactory. Individuals who are unprepared to accept their responsibilities as students and who have demonstrated such should not expect to complete their course of studies. A discussion of the mutual obligations of all members of the academic community is a prerequisite to restoring the academy's balance and clarity of purpose. We began this section with three vignettes which suggested the importance of student responsibility. We conclude with a brief extract from a capstone examination of a graduating college senior who emphasizes the importance of student accountability.

I am ultimately responsible for what happened to me in college. I had to decide whether to get up and go to class and do the readings, or just blow it off. I have learned while I

have been here that I must make the decision to take advan-
tage of opportunities offered to me. You know, sometimes
it isn't easy to say that you have to study or go to the library,
but if you don't then you suffer the consequences. It was
my job to get the most out of my classes, even the boring
ones! Teachers cannot do everything for you, you have to
do the readings and try to make sense of them yourself
(Author's files).

This student's reflections on what it means to go through college reminds us that the challenge for leadership is to understand the dynamics by which institutional efforts can build
student responsibility and to develop policies that promote
students' involvement in their own education. We must nurture an ethic of responsibility and acknowledge students as
equal partners in the relational experience of learning. The
students' contribution to their own college experience and
that of their peers must become more than a tuition check
and an intermittent presence in the classroom. In the following sections we will examine in detail the research that under-
lies the role of student responsibility in promoting positive
collegiate outcomes.

RESPONSIBILITY: Robert Pace's Contribution

Every reform was once a private opinion.
Ralph Waldo Emerson

Quality of Effort

If you were to give one piece of advice to a student who was about to enter college, what would it be? How can a student get the most out of the college years?

Robert Pace would advise the student that learning and development require an investment of time and effort (1982). For students to succeed in college, they must take advantage of all that the college has to offer. This includes utilizing the physical facilities such as science labs, the student union, and the athletic and fine arts areas.

Colleges offer a rich variety of intellectual opportunities. Thus, finding success in college means taking advantage of the social and academic enrichment that comes through informal interactions with faculty and peers, in and out of class. A student's peer relations can, for many, define the college experience. While faculty members can serve as academic helmsmen, the collective energy of all students at the oars actually moves the boat through the water.

Pace defines the investment of time and effort in a college student's studies as "quality of effort" (1982). For him, frequency of activity and consistency of effort are crucially important. To fully take advantage of the library, a student must visit the building and utilize its resources with regularity throughout the school year. In addition, students should use athletic facilities and participate in and attend cultural events sponsored by the institution. To have a meaningful interaction with faculty, showing up is half of success. Academically, a student who never or rarely approaches a professor about issues or assignments simply is not taking responsibility for putting in the time necessary to make the most of the college experience.

If showing up is half of success, the other half is putting effort into the activity. It is a relatively small matter to show up for class regularly but still another to take notes diligently and participate. It is yet another matter to complete additional readings on class topics and apply them in other classes or at work. It is relatively easy to look up a word in a dictionary, yet it takes a good deal more effort to revise a paper two or three times to incorporate the ideas behind the word. The difference between the two is the difference in student effort.

While faculty members can serve as academic helmsmen, the collective energy of all students at the oars actually moves the boat through the water.

Student responsibility means quality of effort, and responsible student behavior is defined by the amount of time a student devotes to high-quality encounters with faculty and peers in and out of class. Amid the current emphasis on accountability and quality, Pace offers a clear-eyed and uncompromising statement of student responsibility:

Colleges are, of course accountable for a lot of things. . . . But surely the students are also accountable for the amount, scope, and quality of effort they invest in their own learning and development (1984, p. 6).

The College Environment

Just as students may be held accountable for their active participation in college life, institutions also have obligations and should be held accountable. As Pace observes, when considering student outcomes one must attend to what the institution offers and what the students do with those offerings. It is unreasonable to expect strong student effort in areas in which the college does not provide appropriate resources. A student can't be expected to develop proficiencies with computers if the college does not provide access to computer equipment and opportunities for high-quality participation with these tools. However, beyond this obvious and important reality lies Pace's 32-year interest in what we now call campus culture or ethos.

Pace recognized the central role the campus environment plays in shaping student effort. A college is responsible for creating a climate that enables students to involve themselves responsibly in college life. In practice this means a clearly articulated and widely understood mission, communicated expectations as seen in rules and policies, a faculty reward structure congruent with stated institutional goals, strong programs and good human relations. In short, the college environment is the sum of its perceived atmosphere (1979).

Pace's recognition of the importance of the collegiate environment found expression in his development, with George Stern, of the College Characteristics Index, or CCI (1958). The CCI is a measure of the "press" of a college, which Stern (1970) describes as the private view of a situation. Collectively, these mutually shared or consensual presses may be taken as a description of an environment.

Ten years later, Pace's thinking was influenced by the work

of Rudolph Moos, who has made extensive and varied studies of a wide variety of environments including college settings (1979). Pace notes that Moos characterized the social climate with three factors: the various goals of the organization; interpersonal relations, especially the degree of emotional support; and the nature of the organization's control or management system, including the relative rigidity and bureaucratization (1984).

When Pace writes about the campus environment or ethos, his thinking reflects the melding of his work with Stern and the contribution of Moos. To Pace, the press of the college environment consists of a variety of possible emphases. These include academic, artistic, analytic, occupational, and personal relevance emphases. Further, a student's interpersonal relationships in college, including those with peers, faculty, and the administration, may be either considerate and supporting or impersonal, remote, and alienated. These twin aspects of the environment, the emphasis and nature of relationships, define, in part, a college's obligations.

Colleges do have a responsibility to clearly articulate their mission. The mission must permeate all aspects of the way the organization deals with its internal and external audiences. The institution has the responsibility to make its facilities comfortable and inviting places. Professors, too, must convey an attitude of approachability, openness, and hospitality inside their classrooms as well as outside. College administrations have a responsibility to create and develop the circumstances in which students and faculty may behave in a facilitative manner with one another. A college administration that fails to create a climate in which teaching and learning can occur optimally has failed its students as badly as if it failed to fund the library.

Student Background

When college students set foot on campus for the first time, they bring with them more than new notebooks and pens. They bring a constellation of differences that increasingly define a pluralistic society. Differences in students' backgrounds help to describe what Pascarella and Terenzini term the conditional effects of college (1991). They are of primary interest to those who wish to study the effect of college on students to determine how the interaction of student behavior and collegiate programs affects learning.

In practice, for a college teacher or administrator, a student's behavior, aptitude, motivation, and learning style are far more important than personal background. As Pace clearly says, "It is possible, although not very probable, that the quality of effort is determined by the chromosomes . . ." (1984, p. 16). From Pace's view, the message is clear and hopeful. It is not *what* students bring to campus that is important—rather, it is *what they do* while they are there that counts. Pace's concern is with "what students do in college, and what conditions in college influence what they do and what they achieve (1984, p. 16).

College Outcomes
What do students learn at college and to what extent can we attribute student outcomes to aspects of the collegiate experience? This seemingly simple question has, over the past half-century or so, led to a remarkable stream of scholarship. It has been the subject of six major reviews, including the landmark review by Feldman and Newcomb (1969), a brace of sweeping analyses by Astin (1977; 1993), a retrospective review by Lenning et al. (1974), a focused review by Pace (1979), and, finally, the work of Pascarella and Terenzini (1991).

It is sufficient at this point to note that college outcomes include more than narrow measures of classroom learning; we will not attempt a comprehensive summary of what constitutes appropriate indicators of college outcomes. The literature simply is too vast for our purposes. Indeed, vocal contributors to the outcomes-assessment movement have been wrestling with these issues for the last 10 years. A broad net of college outcomes recognized by Pace includes personal and social development; gains in general education; cognitive and intellectual outcomes; gains in understanding science and technology; and vocational and career outcomes (1984). These implicitly acknowledge the importance of student development outcomes as well as more conventional academic outcomes. Further, the inclusion of vocational and career gains implies that college outcomes might properly be studied over time.

Summary
Pace's theory about what leads to success in college is straightforward. College outcomes depend on responsible student

behavior. The environment or ethos either may encourage or discourage a student's active participation. While Pace recognizes that students bring to college a diverse set of experiences related to gender, race, and family background, he argues that *what students do while they are enrolled* is more important in affecting student development. The extent to which environment determines outcomes is minimized. The principal contribution to student growth is the extent to which students capitalize on what the college has to offer.

Pace has called his model one of "College Impress." He specifically chose the word "impress" because it connotes a softer impression of the effect of college on students than the term word "impact." Impact implies a powerful and irresistible force, while impress connotes a gentler impression such as a baker might leave on a loaf of bread. The College Impress model suggests that the combined influences of the college environment as perceived by the student and the effort expended by the student lead to student development. It is what the student does in college—rather than the college itself—which is responsible for student gains.

THEORIES OF STUDENT RESPONSIBILITY

No theory is good except on condition that one uses it to go beyond.
Andre Gide

Knowing about theories and theorists is essential if we are to understand student growth and how and why student responsibility must be nurtured. Thomas Kuhn, a philosopher of science, has described the process by which fields of study develop and how, through them, our understanding of the world matures (1970). Initially, descriptions or natural histories of a phenomenon are made. Later, linkages between these descriptive observations are found and theories developed to account for what is observed as well as to guide future research. Over time, difficulties with initial theories accumulate and, ultimately, a large-scale paradigm shift or change in perspective occurs. While there were multi-institutional studies, the first part of this century was dominated by practitioner-based, single-institution studies that lacked integrative theory.

In 1969, Arthur Chickering, writing about higher education studies, observed that "few theories have been framed, few hypotheses tested. Thus, though much useful knowledge has been generated, it remains in unintegrated form" (1969, p. 4). During the next 15 years, about 20 theories, most derived from the field of psychology, were advanced (Terenzini 1987). These theories can be divided into two broad types: developmental theories and college impact theories (Stage 1987; Pascarella and Terenzini 1991).

The developmental theories emphasize the intrapsychic processes which lead to student development and generally contain elaborated descriptions of the sequences or levels of change that a student encounters. The college impact theories, on the other hand, stress the importance of the interaction between individual behavior and environmental presses and emphasize the influences on student change which come from outside of the individual. While Pace specifically avoided characterizing his theory as one of college impact, his work does share the view that change comes about through the interaction of the individual and the environment.

Three other theorists have made contributions to the college impact literature which has largely defined inquiry into college effects for the last 20 years. Vincent Tinto developed the most widely established theory of student departure from college (1975, 1987). Tinto's theory is based on the degree to which students felt integrated into the life of the campus and thus sustained a commitment to graduation. Alexander Astin offered the theory of student involvement and the input-process-output model by which college effects could be analyzed using the national, multi-institutional Cooperative Institutional Research Program (CIRP) data base (1985). Ernest Pascarella offered a generalized causal model to assess college impact which includes measures of institutional features as well as quality of effort (1985, 1991).

Thus, Pace has viewed college outcomes as following from "college impress" and the quality of effort that students put into their work. Looking at the same phenomena, Tinto has seen "student integration," Astin has seen "student involvement," and Pascarella has seen "college impact." In this section we will briefly review and then compare these three theories about how college affects students and learning. These approaches are important, as they directly address the issue of student responsibility.

Tinto and Student Integration
Perhaps the best example of the maturation of college outcomes studies is found in the studies following Tinto's review of the factors associated with student withdrawal from college (1975). Tinto drew for his work on the contributions of Spady (1970, 1971) who emphasized the importance of social integration and path analysis in the study of student retention. Social and academic integration refers to an individual's sense of membership and belonging to an institution.

In Tinto's model, student characteristics such as individual attributes, family background, and pre-college experiences are incorporated into a dynamic model of student departure (1975). These elements lead to an initial commitment to a particular institution and a degree of commitment to completing an academic degree. Over time and through repeated interactions with the academic and social presses of the school, a student's sense of academic and social belonging— or integration—is strengthened or diminished. Specifically, a sense of belonging may be manifested by having college friends, using the college facilities, and actively seeking and receiving counsel from faculty members. The level of integration or belonging that a student experiences subsequently affects the student's commitment to a specific college and the desire to complete the degree. The weaker the student's commitment to an institution or toward degree completion, the greater the likelihood that the student will withdraw from school.

Tinto's model has provided focus and direction for retention research and college outcomes (1975). Among the most prolific and methodologically thorough of those who have worked with Tinto's model are Pascarella and Terenzini (1991). In their watershed review of the literature that describes the effects of college on students, they suggest that Tinto's model, like other "impact models," stresses the importance of environmental and sociological factors in promoting student change. Specifically, they note that "less attention is devoted to specification of the nature or strength of the influences of an institution's structural/organizational characteristics or to the role of individual student effort" (p. 53).

Pascarella and College Impact

While Pascarella and his colleagues have worked extensively with Tinto's model, Pascarella in 1985 developed a generalized model to assess the impact of college on student outcomes. This impact model includes institutional characteristics and student effort, two features lacking in Tinto's formulation. For Pascarella, student learning and development are affected directly by a student's interaction with faculty and peers and by the student's quality of effort, as Pace defines it. The background that a student brings to college may exert a direct influence on collegiate outcomes. However, it is more likely that background will exert an indirect effect, which is mediated by the student's efforts, interactions, and the campus ethos or climate.

From a research perspective, the specification of structural and organizational aspects of an institution (size, resources, governance, etc.) enables researchers who conduct multi-institutional studies to assess the effect these organizational features may have—directly on the college culture, indirectly on student responsibility, and ultimately on college outcomes. Pascarella's college impact model has proved to be a useful tool in the study of patterns of institutional practice as well as in a variety of college outcomes, including affective and intellectual development, self-concept, and civic values and involvement.

Astin and Student Involvement

In the mid-1980s, Astin presented a theory that directly related student involvement to student development and articulated a standard by which colleges could begin to evaluate their programs. For Astin, involvement means the student's investment of "physical and psychological energy" in the academic enterprise. The five principles of his theory are: 1) Involvement refers to the investment of physical and psychological energy; 2) involvement occurs along a continuum that can change over time; 3) involvement has both quantitative and qualitative features; 4) the amount of student learning and personal development associated with any educational program is directly proportional to the quality and quantity of student involvement in that program; and 5) the effectiveness of any educational policy or practice is related directly to the capacity of that policy or practice to increase student involvement. The last two principles are arguably the strongest and most direct calls from the literature to academic leaders to pay attention to the impact their programs have on building student responsibility by encouraging student commitment.

The theory of student involvement has not led to an elaborated model that accounts for student background or explicitly links student behavior to environmental press. Astin wryly notes that he has "not needed to draw a maze consisting of dozens of boxes interconnected by two-headed arrows" to explain his theory to others (1984). The clarity and strength of his propositions have served to guide research in a variety of college settings and for a range of student outcomes. As with Pace, the theory of student involvement explicitly places student behavior at the center of the academic enterprise. Student involvement, like quality of effort, can be described quantitatively (frequency) and qualitatively (depth of commitment).

Although not directly addressed, Astin's theory implies an important role for the college environment. If programmatic success is defined by student involvement, then institutions that develop a climate that supports and nurtures involvement are likely to be successful in building on the strengths students initially bring to the campus. In Astin's terms, these will be institutions of excellence, not because of their reputations or resource base, but because they develop the talents of their students (1985).

Impress, Integration, Impact, and Involvement

Pace, Tinto, Pascarella, and Astin have offered explicit theories about how colleges can promote student learning and growth. Each has left us with a slightly different stance in naming the crucial ingredient. For Pace, it is the quality of effort that students invest in their studies. Tinto argues that, as written in the Talmud, "God resides in the details." Over time and through literally thousands of small interactions with a school's social and academic life, a student's commitment either is strengthened or weakened. Pascarella sees in college outcomes the importance of students' informal interactions with peers and faculty coupled with a high quality of effort. Finally, Astin and the student involvement theory are tightly coupled. For him, student outcomes are directly proportional to student involvement in college activities.

Despite different uses of terms, these approaches have much in common. First, each theorist recognizes that the student's background plays a role in shaping college outcomes. However, that role is largely indirect and moderated by the college environment and a student's interactions with faculty and peers. The good news from these theorists for colleges and students is that the college has a far greater impact on outcomes than the students' backgrounds and background experiences. This holds true only if—and the emphasis is on the word *if*—students take advantage of what the college offers. That is, if the student behaves in a responsible manner.

Second, each sees the campus environment exerting an indirect and potentially enabling impact on college outcomes. For Pace and Pascarella, college climate establishes a tone that is supportive of quality effort and interactions between students, faculty, and peers. Tinto suggests that the fit between the student and the college's social and academic environment shapes the commitment to press on to degree completion. Astin points to the importance of evaluating academic practices and policies in terms of their enabling effect on student involvement.

Last, all emphasize the importance of a partnership between the college and the student. Colleges alone cannot produce student learning. Colleges provide opportunities for interaction and involvement and establish a climate conducive to responsible participation. Yet, in the final analysis, students must extend themselves. Each approach reflects the centrality of what we call student responsibility.

The good news is that the college has a far greater impact on outcomes than the students' backgrounds and background experiences.

While the vision of Pace is clearest, the writings of Tinto, Pascarella, and Astin have stimulated a body of literature that has explored the joint effects of student behavior, campus environment, and student background on college outcomes. The balance of this section examines some of the research literature in each of these three areas as well as the research methodology used in this field.

Methodology

We have spent some energy discussing the contributions that four theorists have made to our understanding of student responsibility. The literature that these theorists have spawned is among the most methodologically sophisticated in the field of higher education. Further, it represents a powerful demonstration of theory coupled with multivariate statistical procedures to bring light to a complex and dynamic social system: our colleges and universities. We will briefly orient the reader to this methodology.

Issues of practice and the current national dialogue concerning student involvement, retention, community building, quality assurance, and accountability all have an intellectual parentage that is based, to some extent, on the body of theory and research that has been developed over the last 20 years. The principal reason that we will consider the developments in methodology is because what we know and what we do not know is dependent on the analytic tools that have been used.

There is a close relationship between our ways of knowing and what we ultimately may conclude from the results of a study. The body of research that undergirds our consideration of student responsibility is a theoretically informed body of scholarship. We believe that only theory-guided research that makes use of appropriate multivariate methodologies has a chance of managing the potentially confounding effects inherent in applied research. Unless we understand the development of this approach, we will be unable to effectively demonstrate the validity of our programs, and senior administrators will be unable to meet the stewardship challenge posed by society.

Competent scholarship spans both theory and methodology. There is a debate on the utility and future direction of research in higher education. Some argue that research should be focused upon specific policy issues of interest to decision makers. Others, including Pascarella, suggest that theory-centered research is an essential component; we too, take the latter position. Theory-centered research is essential to bringing a semblance of coherence to the welter of institutionally based studies. Ultimately, theory-centered research is an exercise in the craft of disciplined sense making. It is a structured, guided process of dialogue with data.

The basic research issues that must be addressed are accounting for gains in college and the threats from student maturation and selection. Students—indeed, all people—grow and change throughout their lifetimes. How can we determine if changes we see in college students are not the result of maturation? Similarly, students self-select and are differentially recruited to different kinds of institutions, majors, and college activities. How can we be sure that college outcomes might not result from the types of students (student background) served rather than college policies or environment?

Classically, the way this has been accomplished in educational research is through experiment, complete with random selection and assignment of student subjects to experimental and control conditions. Randomization equalizes the groups (selection), and random assignment allows us to compare groups with maturation held constant. But colleges are not set up as dreamscapes for researchers. They are applied settings. And we know, up front, that the college-going group is very different from the noncollege-going group; that different people attend different types of institutions; and that different people selectively participate in varied activities, in different majors, and different micro-environments while at college. So we have several confounding variables (alternate hypotheses) that always are tenable in research of this kind. These include individual background, aptitude, prior academic history, social and economic background, personality, and other elements which become entangled with college experience and college outcome.

During the last 25 years, a series of approaches to managing these problems has been utilized. Early studies typically ignored these difficulties and focused instead on descriptions of student behavior and reported practices that presumably were effective on individual campuses. In the late '60s and into the '70s, researchers began to use correlation-based techniques which sought to statistically control for selection effects by holding constant or partialling out initial student differences. Unfortunately, this approach did not explain the sources of influence on college outcomes. With a large number of variables held constant, any college effect can appear artificially small. In the mid-'70s and into the early '80s, multiple regression analysis was used extensively and indeed, stepwise procedures still are important analytic tools. The principal contribution that multiple regression makes is an estimate of the relative effect of each predictor variable on the outcome (response) variable. Statistically, these effects are expressed as standardized beta weights. By effect, researchers mean the direct, unmediated contribution that knowledge of one variable (a predictor) makes to accounting for an outcome variable. For example, if we wished to study the effects of student age, effort, and perception of college environment on student gains in general knowledge, we could use multiple regression analysis to assess the relative contribution that each predictor (age, effort, perception) made in accounting for the magnitude of student gains.

In regression, effects are expressed as standardized beta weights. Interpreting standardized betas allows us to assess the relative effect or contribution of a predictor compared to other predictors within a given sample. For example, we enter the predictors into the regression analysis in a theoretically consistent manner (age, then perception, and finally effort) and determine that the effect of age (standardized beta) is .07; perception is .11; and effort is .57. We can conclude that the contribution of age and perception, while statistically significant, is relatively slight—especially when compared to the contribution that effort makes in accounting for gains. Indeed, it can be said that the effect of effort is more than five times that of either age or perception. Further, we can say that the net effect of effort on gains is quite powerful. That is, after accounting for age and perception, the contribution of effort still is the most important factor. While regression analysis proved to be a major advance, it still was primarily predictive in nature rather than an explanation of the process by which mediating variables could moderate the effect of entry variables on outcomes.

During the late '70s and through the mid-'80s, an approach known as path analysis, causal modeling, or structural modeling offered several advantages and largely replaced regression analysis in the study of college outcomes. The most important of these advantages is the ability to model a priori causal structures; that is, to represent theoretically derived systems in a statistically expressible form. Causal models based on path analysis also allow the user to identify direct, indirect, and total effects of model elements on outcomes measures. Direct effects in path analysis have the same meaning as standardized betas in regression. Indirect effects refer to the mediated impact that one variable may have on a third variable. Total effects simply are the sum of the contribution of the direct and indirect effects.

We might imagine a model based on Pace's work. In this imaginary model, the variables that exert a direct effect on gains in general education are perception of the college environment and student effort. It is possible for the total effect of a variable to be zero yet have relatively strong direct and indirect effects. For example, age may exert a positive direct effect on general education outcomes because adult students have a greater fund of general knowledge than younger students. Yet, it may exert a negative effect on effort in college, possibly due to competing demands from job and family. The positive effect of prior knowledge thus is rendered nugatory by the negative effect of work and family demands.

The use of path analysis offers major advantages over regression but requires strong theory to support the initial model specification. It has been said that there are two parts to path modeling: the easy part and the hard part. The easy part is the solution of the multiple equations via computer analyses, and the hard part is the initial model specification based upon sound theory with variables that are well-measured.

Despite the advantages of path analysis, there are several problems. The first is the assumption that the relationships among the variables are unidirectional. In the real world it is not always possible to rule out reciprocal or looping relationships. In the above example, there may be a reciprocal relationship between effort and perception. That is, a positive perception of the college could lead to the expenditure of effort, while the expenditure of effort might lead students to see the college in a favorable light. The model we posed above suggests a one-way flow, and with path analysis we are limited to posing unidirectional causal chains.

The second and most vexing problem is the assumption that the variables of interest are measured without error. That is, we assume we are dealing with reality rather than measured constructs. Typically, prior to a path analysis or regression analysis, variables (constructs) are factored to produce relatively homogeneous scales with acceptable measures of internal consistency (reliability) and validity (construct validity).

From the mid-'80s to the present we have seen the application of covariance structure analysis approaches such as linear structural relations, or LISREL (Joreskog and Sorbom 1988), and EQS (Bentler 1989). These approaches allow us to specify reciprocal relationships and, most importantly, to specify a measurement model attached to the path or structural model. This allows the estimation of effects uncontaminated by measurement error, as effects are specified or included in the model itself. As with path analysis, these approaches allow for the specification of direct and indirect effects and the testing of relationship paths as well as tests of the adequacy of the entire model as specified.

The reader interested in an accessible and complete treatment of the evolution in the methodology of college outcomes research is urged to review the appendix of Pascarella and Terenzini's review volume (1991). Astin makes use of multiple regression analysis, and the first three chapters of his book, *What Matters in College*, walk the reader through the application of this procedure (1993). While covariance structure modeling can be formidable to master, the interested reader is encouraged to review Baldwin for an excellent applied introduction to this approach using LISREL (1989). Stage offers a primer on the use of causal analysis technique and offers suggestions for applications of LISREL for research on college students (1989).

RESEARCH ON STUDENT BACKGROUND

Character—the willingness to accept responsibility for one's own life—is the source from which self-respect springs.
Joan Didion

The four theoretical perspectives we have examined all suggest that a student's personal background characteristics are less important in determining college outcomes than are the student's experiences and behavior while enrolled. The studies we will review in this section constitute one of the most theoretically grounded literatures in the field and are largely derived from the thinking of Pace, Tinto, Pascarella, and Astin.

In these studies we see a general progression from the use of multiple regression analysis to the use of causal models which allow the researcher to tease out the direct and indirect effects of student background variables on outcomes. Further, smaller, single-institution based samples have been replaced by very large-scale, multi-institutional data bases. The state of the art in this field now includes theoretically derived causal modeling using nationally generalizable samples. This powerful mix of theory, method, and sample has added to our understanding of the role personal student background characteristics play in interactions with the college environment and student behavior.

Numerous outcomes have been examined including retention, freshman-year persistence, plans for graduate school, personal development, and academic achievement. A wide variety of student background variables also have been studied, including race, age, gender, family background, socio-economic status, parental aspirations and support, high school achievement, and individual intrapsychic characteristics. Most of the studies have attempted to hold constant or net out the effect of background variables by including them directly in the models. Other studies have examined the differential effects of selected background variables by running separate models for specific groups and then comparing the workings (effect structures) of each resulting model. This makes direct comparisons between studies with differing approaches difficult yet fruitful.

For most researchers, two questions about background variables are important. The first question concerns the process by which background affects student gains (directly on outcomes or indirectly through process variables) and second, determining the comparative magnitude of the effect when placed alongside other variables such as student-faculty interaction, intentions, aspirations, or quality of effort. We shall review some of these studies, beginning with the methodologically less sophisticated and proceeding to the more recent and methodologically advanced ones which were able to control for numerous variables.

Pace, in a study of eight colleges with a total of 2,299 students who took the College Student Experiences Questionnaire (CSEQ), reports that in the five categories of student gains measured, the most pervasive predictor was the quality of effort that students put into their studies (1984). When variables were entered into a regression analysis in a setwise order with student background variables entered first, they accounted for a very small percent (less than 5 percent) of the variation in gains. Quality of effort variables were entered into the equations last and accounted for the largest proportion of variation in gains (between 5 and 25 percent) even after accounting for student background.

While Pace's study suggests a limited although statistically significant role for student background characteristics, it has two major limitations. First, separate analyses for particular subgroups are not offered, making comparisons between groups difficult. Second, an interaction hypothesis which could shed light on the conditional effects of effort was not specified.

Some 11 years after the initial publication of the CSEQ, Pace presented a major descriptive portrait of American college students based on the responses of 25,000 students enrolled at 74 colleges between the years 1983-86 (1990). The book, titled *The Undergraduates*, presents a series of student snapshots concerning their college experience. Among the analyses presented is a description of student activities by ethnicity, age, and gender. Pace reports that there are "no major differences between any of the groups (white, black, Hispanic, Asian) on the scholarly, intellectual activities, or on the informal, interpersonal activities" (1990, p. 86). In areas related to science and technology, Asian students had a slightly higher participation (3 percent) than did black students. Asians reported the lowest participation in athletics and involvement in clubs, while blacks rated highest in use of the Student Union and participation in clubs.

When the data is disaggregated by age, the oldest group of students, aged 28 and up, appear less likely to take advantage of either college group facilities or informal interpersonal activities with other students. Their participation in the academic life of the campus, however, is at least as strong and, in the case of class-specific activities, stronger, than their younger counterparts. These findings are consistent with other methodologically sophisticated studies which report that older and commuter students are more fully engaged in the academic life of the campus than in the social dimension.

Finally, Pace reports an absence of educationally significant differences between men and women in college activities participation. There is a slight trend, however, for women to report making more progress in personal and social development. In sum, while there are some differences between demographically defined groups of students, these are relatively slight and are largely overshadowed by what the groups have in common.

While noticeable differences in social participation between older and younger students were apparent, Pace concludes that "the quality of effort invested in various college activities and the progress claimed toward various goals was relatively similar for each gender and each ethnic group" (1990, p. 139). These findings are largely, but not fully, consistent with other studies that statistically control for student demographic characteristics.

In a single-institution longitudinal study of student intellectual skill development, Terenzini, Theophilides, and Lorang found that only students' level of classroom participation was consistently related to growth (1984). Further, their findings suggested that growth was associated with nonclassroom interaction with faculty. Factors such as sex, parents' education, SAT scores, and highest degree planned did not statistically affect academic skill development. Only high school rank significantly contributed to freshman-year academic skill development, but even this did not contribute to development in subsequent years.

In a similar, single-institution study of transfer student intellectual skill development, Volkwein, King, and Terenzini found that student background and prior college activities were singularly unimportant in accounting for student intellectual growth (1986). In this study, which used multiple regression analysis, the records of 3,000 undergraduates entering the State University of New York at Albany in 1980 were analyzed. The key to student intellectual growth, the researchers found, was not age, sex, prior education, and goals, but the perception that faculty are devoted teachers. This sense of devotion includes aspects such as intellectually stimulating class sessions, encouraging students to express their views, and spending time outside of class discussing intellectual issues of interest to students.

Using data collected as part of the Cooperative Institutional Research Program (CIRP), Astin completed a massive study of college impact (1993). This study, reported in *What Matters in College*, analyzes the responses of more than 27,000 students at hundreds of colleges across the United States Astin uses the I-E-O model, or Input-Environment-Outcomes model, to analyze college effects. Making use of regression models, he assembled over 146 input measures which tap a wide variety of student characteristics at time of the student's initial enrollment. Astin assesses the contribution of the college's environment to the change in students, beyond what can be predicted from initial student characteristics. Unfortunately, as he notes, separate analyses were not completed by race, gender, ability of student, or socioeconomic status (SES). This makes it difficult to determine any interaction effects or other subgroup differences. The strength of the study lies in its breadth of measures used and strength of the national sample.

Astin, in this study, found statistically significant effects on most college outcomes measures of student demographic characteristics including race, gender, and socioeconomic status (1993). He concluded that "the student's peer group is the single most potent source of influence on growth and development during the undergraduate years" (p. 398). All students, irrespective of age, gender, and social and economic background, come to college with preexisting differences. Yet, these students likely will develop in the direction of the dominant values of their college peers. In short, student involvement with peers mediates change.

As indicated previously, regression studies did not examine any possible conditional effects of student background characteristics. Although primarily concerned with examining the role of academic and social integration in persistence, Pascarella and Terenzini tested a set of interaction hypotheses between sex, race, initial college enrollment, aptitude, and five student academic and social integration scales (1980). Of the 20 interaction terms tested in a discriminant function analysis, only two were significant. These were sex by peer-group interaction and sex by institution and goal commitment. The quality of peer-group interaction is more important in women's decisions to persist or withdraw than it is for men. Conversely for men, their level of commitment to degree goals and the institution are more strongly tied to their persistence.

While this study suggested possible indirect effects that student background variables may exert, it was Munro who first demonstrated this phenomenon using path analysis (1981). This procedure has two major advantages over most regression-based approaches. First, the researcher can test detailed, theoretically based models; second, the direct and indirect effects of variables can be determined.

Barbara Munro developed a path analytic model based on Tinto's work (1981). She used the NLS-72 data set which is a nationwide, longitudinal study of the high school class of 1972. Her interest was to develop and test a model which directly would examine the interaction of student personal characteristics with the collegiate environment. Following Tinto, she selected student retention as her outcome variable. Her findings suggest that the effects of SES, ethnicity, and sex on persistence in college are mainly indirect and transmitted through intervening variables such as academic and social integration. Indeed, the only student background variable that exerts a direct effect on persistence is high school grades. Thus, the degree to which the students are academically and socially integrated into the life of the campus is more important in accounting for retention outcomes than are the initial personal student characteristics.

For women, social integration had a stronger effect on persistence than academic integration.

Several studies have developed and tested theoretically derived causal models for men and women separately. Pascarella and Terenzini, in a path analytic study based on Tinto's model, found important differences when the sample was disaggregated by sex (1983). For women, social integration had a stronger effect on persistence than academic integration. For men, academic integration was more important, while the effects of social integration were indirect, transmitted through institutional commitment. They note that the influence of student preenrollment characteristics (family background, individual attributes, pre-college schooling) was indirect, and the effect of these variables on persistence was mediated by the freshman-year experience. For residential students, the quality of student interaction with the college environment was more important in persistence decisions than the characteristics brought to college.

This study is important, as it reflects a more complete specification of the variables in Tinto's model than had previously been attempted. As a longitudinal study, it reflects the commitments that students have at different points in time. Unfortunately, it is a single institution study with all subjects drawn from a "large, independent, residential university in central New York state." Thus, suggestive as these findings are, we cannot generalize these results to other institutional types or different student populations.

Based on the above research which suggested the importance of sex differences, Stoecker, Pascarella, and Wolfle developed and tested four sex-by-race causal models, including models for black and white men and women (1988). The sample was drawn from data obtained from the CIRP. More than 10,000 students enrolled at 487 colleges and universities of various types initially were included in the study. Using the methodology of causal modeling, they implemented Tinto's model and, following the work of Pascarella, added institutional characteristics (1985). They found that when controlling for the influence of all other variables in the model, academic integration had the strongest direct effect on persistence for all four sex-by-race groups. Further, social integration, including interactions with faculty and social leadership, had positive effects on persistence. They conclude by noting that "student affairs programs that facilitate interaction with faculty and the opportunity for social involvement and participation would seem to positively influence persistence irrespective of pre-college characteristics; initial commitments; the selectivity; size or racial composition of the institution attended; or one's academic major" (p. 205).

James Hearn, in a multi-institutional path analytic study based on the work of Pascarella (1985), examined student aspirations and plans for graduate education (1987). Hearn developed two submodels: one for men and one for women. He found that for graduating women, the roles of academic performance and major were less important than for men, but the role of parental supportiveness was more important. For men and women, the role of the background factors for both types of outcomes was significant but largely indirect. Of caution is the finding that the developed and tested model appeared to fit the male subsample better than it did the female subsample. This suggests that important variables, unaccounted for in the model, may be exerting a differential effect on women's future plans for schooling. While this finding is intriguing, they conclude by reminding us that "choices made by educational leaders do matter" (p. 137). Features of the college environment that can be affected by administrators do influence subsequent career plans and aspirations beyond what students bring to the collegiate setting.

While it is not our purpose here to examine in any detail the growing body of literature being developed around the issues of race or ethnicity and college outcomes, we are reminded of the scholarship of Fleming (1984) and others who have expressly examined this question. Inarguably, in the single most sustained and comprehensive examination of the black experience at "white" and "black" colleges across the country, Fleming examined a diverse range of academic, cognitive, psychological, and developmental features of the black student experience. She concludes that at "white" institutions, academic achievement is thwarted by poor adjustment of black students to the "white" campus, especially with respect to the faculty.

Similar findings were reported by Suen, who examined the relationship between alienation among minority students and attrition (1983). Crosson suggests that a key ingredient in improving minority achievement and retention is in the promotion of involvement in campus life (1988). Oliver describes a study completed at the University of California at Los Angeles of black and Chicano achievement and social adjustment (1985). The study suggests that reported feelings of alienation and isolation on the campus adversely affect student achievement.

Nettles, working within the tradition of Astin and Pascarella, attempted to compare directly the performance of white and black students by taking into account a wide range of institutional and student/faculty interaction factors (1991). In a large-scale study of 30 colleges, 700 faculty members, and more than 4,000 students, separate multiple regression analyses were conducted on the responses of white and black students. Of especial interest is the finding that "black students also have lower academic integration, more limited contact with faculty outside of the classroom, and more faculty who are dissatisfied with their universities" (p. 90). Nettles speculates that the comparatively less-satisfied faculty who teach

black students may contribute to lower levels of black-student involvement through diminished levels of student-faculty interaction.

While considerable interest has been devoted to exploring the implication of certain personal characteristics of students on college outcomes, very little attention has been devoted to the participation rates or process of college-going for individuals with disabilities. The passage of the Americans with Disabilities Act has heightened issues of access and participation for the disabled in postsecondary institutions, and we anticipate a body of much-needed theoretically centered research.

Fairweather and Shaver made creative and effective use of two national longitudinal data sets to describe the enrollment rates in postsecondary education for college-aged youths with and without disabilities (1990). Their study used the National Transition Study, a data set containing a five-year followup of 6,877 disabled youths and the High School and Beyond data set. Items common to the two sets permitted comparisons in the participation rates for disabled and nondisabled groups. The findings indicate that the college-going rate for disabled vs. nondisabled individuals is somewhat more than 1-to-2 for two-year colleges and 1-to-10 for four-year colleges. Of substantial interest is the finding that there is considerable variation within groups comprising individuals with different disabilities. The two-year college enrollment rate for deaf, speech-impaired, other health-impaired, and those with visual and aural deficits was roughly comparable to that of nonimpaired individuals. As further efforts at accommodation, mandated by law, are made, it is likely that the participation rates in four-year colleges will continue to rise.

With the rise in college-going rates, researchers in several studies have sought to understand the attrition of the disabled by turning to the model of school-leaving advanced by Tinto. Walter and Welsh (1986) and Walter and DeCaro (1986) argue that depending on its nature and severity, the impairment of disabled students may impose unique barriers to their academic and social integration into the life of the college. They call upon individual institutions to collect and analyze institutional research data to identify and suggest attrition interventions for the disabled.

Following on the call for an implementation of Tinto's model, Scherer, Stinson, and Walter conducted a causal analysis based on elements of Tinto's theory (1987). In a one-year longitudinal study of 233 students enrolled at the National Technical Institute for the Deaf, the researchers found that social integration was a key variable in the retention of deaf students. Social satisfaction had a positive impact on retention, while participation in college-sponsored activities had a negative effect. The latter finding is not surprising and may be accounted for by the unique needs that this institution serves. Many hearing-impaired students arrive in college with important unmet needs for social participation. Extensive participation in college activities may undermine a student's ability to complete needed academic obligations.

Clearly, these findings suggest that there are common underlying processes in the persistence decisions of the disabled and the nondisabled. Future research using causal methodology and multi-institutional data sets, informed by a theoretical perspective, is surely needed and will illuminate our understanding of the impact of disabilities on the relations between college environment and disabled students.

Summary and Retrospective

We understand this emerging and still underdeveloped body of knowledge as underscoring the centrality of active student involvement on campus and in the classroom. The literature is consistent with that derived from the theoretical traditions of Pace, Pascarella, Tinto, and Astin in that it minimizes the contribution of any personal student characteristics to college outcomes. It further illustrates the importance of examining the interaction of background characteristics with the college environment and student behavior. Both students and institutions have mutual obligations to one another. The literature reminds us that ethnicity, gender, age, disability, and other personal attributes do not present an insurmountable barrier to satisfactory college outcomes.

Institutions have an obligation to promote a climate that facilitates student involvement and interaction. Students must be responsible partners with colleges and extend themselves to take advantage of the opportunities that are offered. Through encounters with each other, faculty, staff, and the curriculum, a sense of mutuality and community can be developed.

As this country struggles toward some still unclear reconciliation with our past and searches for the basis of hope for the future when we deal with issues of race, gender, class, and ability, we stroke wounds that have not yet been bound up. In our desire for knowledge, our use of methods such as causal modeling and large-scale aggregate statistics may seem to distance us from people. As Parker Palmer cautions us, if our passion to know springs from mere "amoral curiosity" or from a thirst for power over others, that knowledge ultimately will poison us and salt our enterprise (1983).

We must keep in mind that compassion for our students and love of our enterprise require conflict and the vigorous discourse that accompanies the search for truth both individual and collective. Our students must become our partners in that search. The research base that we have reviewed suggests that all students, irrespective of their backgrounds, can and do learn on our campuses and in our classrooms *if* they take responsibility for their own behavior within the context of an institution that actively promotes student involvement in learning.

COLLEGE ENVIRONMENT

Great schools are little societies.
H. Fielding

In this section we will consider the interrelationship between the college environment, what students do while enrolled, and college outcomes. In describing the characteristics of a college or university, two broad and complementary sets of features must be considered. First, a college can be described physically, organizationally, and demographically. What is its size? Is it a residential or commuter school? What are the gender and racial compositions? These are the formal and readily quantified characteristics of an institution, but there are other factors too. For instance, if all you knew about a person was height, color of hair, and age, you would know very little about that person as an individual. To understand what makes people tick, one has to understand their psychological makeup, values, attitudes, and personality. So it is with institutions.

The second feature that must be accounted for in describing an institution is its psychological or cultural feel. While this institutional characteristic is no less important than its demographic features, it is more difficult to define and measure quantitatively. By "feel," we refer to the important psychological dimension of an institution's climate. Is the campus open and accessible in a human sense, or do people feel alienated and disconnected? Are students transients on the campus? Do faculty feel a sense of community? Finally, is the climate one that communicates a sense of purpose, or is there a cacophony of voices—or worse, simply a silence concerning the larger mission of the institution?

While there may be no connection between a person's character and physical features, for institutions there is a link between the formal characteristics and its character or psychological feel. Moos, who influenced Pace's thinking on the role of the collegiate environment, suggests that the college environment consists of three interacting building blocks (1979). These are the 1) physical arrangements of the campus; 2) organizational factors including size, governance system, and resources; and 3) the human aggregate. The human aggregate can be considered the collective norms of the institution: Is it a "party" school? Do students study on weekends? Do students actively participate in campus organizations? Do faculty have an open-door policy with regard to students, or do students make appointments a week in advance? This normative aspect of the college environment, reinforced by the physical arrangements and organizational features, creates a campus social climate through which individuals experience the college. Thus, the campus climate mediates and is shaped by the structural aspects of the collegiate environment.

Pace, too, argues that the institution's environment or ethos is a shaping force and stimulus for student development (1979). While affirming the importance of individual students' responsibility for their own efforts in learning, Pace argues that "environmental characteristics make up the institutional context and the stimulus for the amount, scope, and quality of students' effort" (p. 128).

Astin's recognition of the importance of environment was marked at least as early as the 1968 publication of his book *The College Environment.* He reports the results of a survey of student activities at more than 200 colleges and universities and stresses the impact upon achievement-related behaviors, self-esteem, and feelings of isolation and alienation that may result from mismatches between the student and the environment. In this, he presages the work of Tinto with his emphasis on the importance of the degree of fit between the individual and the institution. In fact, while individual integration into the life of the institution largely determines outcomes, it is "a person's normative and structural integration into the academic and social systems" that leads to retention and degree completion outcomes (1975, p. 96).

In his General Causal Model of student development, Pascarella suggests both the mediating effects of the formal organizational characteristics (size, selectivity, percent residential) of the environment and the institutional environment or culture (1985). For him, the college climate mediates the effect of college structure on the quality of student effort as well as shapes the extent of student-peer and student-faculty interactions.

The literature suggests that the college environment consists of two components: formal organizational characteristics and college culture. Organizational characteristics shape the social environment and are believed to affect student behavior and, thus, college culture. In this section, we will follow the research evidence that links the college characteristics and environment with student responsibility and college outcomes.

Institutional Size

In the aftermath of the student demonstrations of the late 1960s, many in the academy were shocked at the extent of the breach between students and the collegium. In the search for an explanation, some turned to factors associated with the nature of the formal organization itself, especially its size and the potential for alienation that mass societies, in general, produce. Clark, in a description of large research universities, noted that while "technical data" and "facts" might be taught en masse by "impersonal means," the larger effects of education on the "mind and character of students will be weak" (1962). Hall and Kehoe, in a superb reflection on student unrest and its sociological causes, identify institutional size itself as the principal source of the rift between students and the academy (1971). As they say:

> To summarize, the massification of the university produces two major trends that inhibit the educational process. The first is the impersonalization of the communication process in learning situations and the second is the reeducation of motivational support on the part of both students and faculty for the direct, involved exchange that learning demands (p. 66).

They recommend a series of reforms that are intended to create intervening structures that can mediate between the mass institution and the student and promote a sense of community and relatedness among members of the university. Unfortunately for the academy, the changes they hoped to promote were never instituted on a large scale. Indeed, they conclude their article on a somewhat pessimistic note. They imply that short-term changes that have been adopted in response to the student protests of the 1960s have not resulted in substantive institutional change in structure or in the value system of the university.

In a similar vein, Smith and Bernstein, in the book *The Impersonal Campus*, suggest that to provide a high-quality undergraduate educational experience, most public colleges and universities have simply become too large (1979). They also advocate trying out a range of intermediate structures and services that are intended to reintegrate students within the body of the academy. Their recommendations for the establishment of mediating structures, such as cluster colleges and other smaller-scale or human-scale integrative opportunities, are well-grounded in experience and theory.

What does the research on the effect of size on college outcomes indicate? In an 11-institution survey of more than 2,000 freshmen, Pascarella and Chapman found that in a series of path analytic models, the effect of institutional size on persistence in college was relatively slight and indirect through its effect on academic and social integration (1983). Chapman and Pascarella, in a subsequent detailed reanalysis of the multi-institutional data set used by Pascarella and Chapman (1983), report that institutional size accounts for only a slight proportion of variation in students' academic and social integration. Further, at large institutions rather than smaller schools, students tend to report greater use of campus-based opportunities for social encounters. Unfortunately, however, size also appears to inhibit interaction with faculty, both by distancing students and faculty in informal out-of-class interactions and in more formal academic matters as well.

Institutional size, however, does influence student affective development. Astin, in his massive analysis of CIRP data collected at more than 400 institutions, reports that institutional size exerts substantial, largely negative but indirect effects on student affective development, the perception that faculty care about students, and general satisfaction with the quality of instruction (1993). Unfortunately, size appears to positively affect a student's view that the only purpose of college is to increase one's economic well-being, and that the individual can do little to change society.

The literature appears consistent and suggests that institutional size does exert a small and negative, but reliable, indirect effect on the propensity of students and faculty to engage one another around academic issues. Further, through its tendency to isolate students, institutional size can interfere in the creation of a climate or ethos which supports student responsibility and thus undermines academic achievement, student development, and retention. A line of inquiry which parallels and is confounded by size is the effect of institutional type on college outcomes.

Institutional Type
It is apparent that institutions with their differing missions, facilities, and collective pasts convey to students and faculty different sets of expectations and thus have a distinct cultural

feel. The first question that arises, then, is how are institutional types defined? In the literature, institutions have been mapped by gender (male and female institutions), race (historically black colleges, Native American colleges), and religious affiliation (Catholic, Protestant, Baptist, Jewish). We also might consider public and private secular institutions as a typologies dimension. Within the context of student responsibility, two typologies are especially pertinent: one that examines institutional type by Carnegie classification (research, doctoral, comprehensive, selective, and general liberal arts, community college) and the other, which examines institutional type by the location/modal residence of the students (commuter/residential).

Pace, in the book *The Undergraduates*, presents a descriptive comparison of the responses of more than 25,000 undergraduates enrolled at 74 colleges and universities nationwide (1990). These students completed the College Student Experiences Questionnaire (CSEQ) during the years 1983 to 1986. From this large but nonrandom sampling, Pace disaggregated student responses by Carnegie type and examined, by institutional type, the ways in which students engaged in activities. When students go to college, do they engage in a common core of activities which center around scholarly and intellectual activities and informal interpersonal activities? Pace found that at least 90 percent of all students interacted with faculty, took notes, thought about learning applications, and had conversations with students of different backgrounds about music, popular culture, course work, and the comments of professors.

Pace also found that students at liberal arts institutions differed from those at other types of institutions. In nearly all cases, it was the selective liberal arts colleges that reported the highest levels of participation in a wide range of academic and social activities. The students at research and doctoral universities reported the lowest rates of high-quality participation in academic and peer activities. Indeed, Pace argues that at those institutions which enroll the vast majority of American college students (research, doctoral, and comprehensive institutions), there is very little variation in the behavior of students. It is only within the selective liberal arts colleges that student participation reaches a noticeably different and higher level.

Another study of the impact of college type on student activity also made use of student responses to the CSEQ

The students at research and doctoral universities reported the lowest rates of high-quality participation in academic and peer activities.

(Baird 1990). Baird used data collected at seven doctoral universities, four comprehensive colleges, six selective liberal arts colleges, 12 general liberal arts colleges, and 13 community colleges. His findings confirm those reported by Pace, in which both selective and general liberal arts college students reported the highest engagement in social and academic activities (1990). Of interest was the strong involvement of community college students in writing activities and yet very limited involvement in college activities outside of the formal classroom setting. Except for the liberal arts students, much of what has been considered involvement in the general life of the campus appears limited.

Unfortunately, the possible confounding effect of residency on institutional type was not addressed either by Pace (1990) or Baird (1990). It might be that the distinctive effects found in these studies for the liberal arts institutions could be accounted for by student opportunities for involvement, rather than to the type of institution.

Pascarella and Chapman (1983) and Chapman and Pascarella (1983) include measures of institutional type and commuter status (two-year commuter, four-year commuter, four-year residential) in their path analytic study of retention at 11 postsecondary institutions. Of interest is their finding that at residential institutions, persistence was directly affected by social engagement, but in two- and four-year commuter settings, academic integration was indirectly related to persistence through its direct effects on institutional commitment. That is, at commuter institutions, those students who persisted did so because their ties to the college were strengthened in the classroom setting.

A further finding concerns the role of individual student background variables such as sex, age, and class. At the residential four-year institutions, the effect of these factors on persistence was indirect and largely mediated by social integration. At the two- and four-year commuter institutions, these background factors exerted a direct and unmediated effect on persistence. These findings suggest that commuter schools, especially those that fail to develop mediating social networks for their commuter students, may in fact simply "pass through" their students without affecting them in any substantial way. Commuter students, especially those from disadvantaged backgrounds, who do not participate in potentially mediating out-of-class social contacts with peers and faculty ultimately may not learn how to take full advantage of all the college offers, particularly in the area of personal development. Perhaps the high levels of participation reported by Pace (1990) and Baird (1990) may be attributed to the social mediation available to residential students in smaller, more personal institutional contexts.

If, as we have seen, the nature of the commuter experience limits the impact that an institution has on students and places a premium on the contact that commuter students enjoy in the classroom, then we should consider a line of research that has developed around the commuter experience and commuter institution.

Residential and Commuter Institutions

Two of the earliest large-scale national studies that sought to untangle the mix of institutional type, residency status, and student background were by Chickering and Kuper (1971) and Astin (1973). Focusing on 13 liberal arts colleges—some predominantly residential, others predominantly commuter— Chickering and Kuper found important differences in the backgrounds of commuter and residential students. It was the great divide between the haves and the have-nots. Parents of residential students were wealthier and their children had better high school grades, higher aspirations, higher test scores, broader interests, and broader purposes in their reasons for pursuing a college degree. The effect of residency or commuter status was to exaggerate rather than to reduce the initial background differences. Citing the Bible, Chickering and Kuper say "to them who had more, was given; from them who had less, was taken away (p. 259). Arguing from a developmental perspective, Chickering and Kuper speculate that dormitory living provides students with challenges for independent living that cannot be met by living at home. They further argue that campus residential situations can serve as intermediating units between the college, the external "establishment," and the student. These residential units and "the cultures they represent are the principal developmental agents for college students" (p. 260).

Astin reports a series of multiple regression analyses of CIRP data collected between 1966 and 1970 on more than 25,000 students at 213 institutions (1973). His findings confirm those of Chickering and Kuper concerning the positive effect of dormitory living on retention. Recognizing the confounding of institutional type with residency status, Astin analyzed institutional type and residency status and found that at four-year colleges and universities, the chance of degree completion in four years is enhanced by leaving home. In two-year colleges, the completion rates were uniformly low regardless of whether the student lived in a dorm, at home, or in a private residence.

The findings of Astin (1973) and Chickering and Kuper were confirmed in a single-institution study of older commuter students enrolled at a large research university (Copland-Wood 1985). In another study of older commuter students at six metropolitan (commuter) universities, Arnold et al. utilized CSEQ data from more than 3,000 students (1991). They were concerned with the relative contribution of environmental factors and student quality of effort factors in accounting for student self-reported gains. In most cases, the effect of age, while negatively related to gains, was slight, while perceptions of the environment exerted an effect at least as important. The most consistently potent factor in accounting for a range of personal, academic, and vocational gains was the effort that students put into their own studies and their interpersonal on-campus relationships.

Two studies made use of statistical models derived from Tinto's model of student withdrawal from college. In a path analytic study of students enrolled at 11 two- and four-year institutions, Pascarella and Chapman (1983) controlled for student background and institutional type. They found that living on campus had a direct and an indirect effect (through social integration) on persistence. For the commuter institutions, naturally, the benefits of on-campus residency were not available. In a recent causal analysis of the collegiate experience of almost 1,000 students enrolled at six metropolitan commuter institutions, Glover implemented a model of student gains using the Tinto constructs of academic and social integration (1992). In her analysis, student background characteristics did not contribute directly to the model. Only the degree of a student's academic integration contributed to gains in general education.

In retrospect, the synthesis offered by Hall and Kehoe (1971) and the early studies of Chickering and Astin appear to have been confirmed by a consistent, though complex, series of subsequent studies. The formal features of a college, including its size, type, and residential character, appear to exert a small but consistent effect on student outcomes. Large-sized institutions, without effective mediating units, and those that offer little opportunity for out-of-class social interaction between students and peers and students and faculty, tend to be less efficacious in affecting positive student outcomes or retaining students to a timely degree completion. While it is clearly possible for students to obtain a satisfactory education at these institutions, students who persist and expend high-quality effort in their academic work are more likely than others to acquire a good education. This places a premium on developing within students the sense of responsibility for their own learning at just those schools at which the atmosphere for doing so is the weakest. In the next section, we will examine the nature of institutional ethos or environment and its effect on student effort and responsibility.

The College Environment
Each of the four principal theorists has emphasized the role of college environment in enhancing student outcomes. For Pace, the college environment encompasses the physical arrangements that contribute to student participation as well as the role that the campus ethos plays in shaping students' efforts. Thus, the campus environment is the sum of its perceived atmosphere. This atmosphere either can promote student effort or discourage students from investing themselves in the life of the campus. In Tinto's model of student retention, satisfactory college outcomes occur when, over time and through countless repetitive encounters with the social and academic features of the campus, an individual's sense of belonging or commitment to an institution is strengthened or degraded. Institutional commitment then is a central causal component in his model.

Tinto (1975) reasons that central to his model of student withdrawal is "the notion that perceptions of reality have real effects on the observer . . . it is the perceptions of the individual that are important" (p. 98). The level of belonging that a student experiences subsequently affects the student's commitment to a specific college and generally affects the desire to press on to degree completion. In Pascarella's model, the institution's environment may indirectly affect college outcomes through its shaping effect on the quality of student effort and the frequency and quality of faculty and peer interactions with students. The nature of the campus environment,

in turn, is shaped by the formal features of the college (size, type, percent residential, selectivity) and the backgrounds of the students who are admitted. In Astin's theory of student involvement, institutional policies and practices are shaped by the extent to which they promote students' involvement in their studies.

Each of these theorists sees a facilitating role for the campus environment. A crucial feature of each of these varied but related approaches is the students' sense or perception that they are in a place that supports learning in general and their personal learning and growth in particular. The term "environment," or "ethos," is a very broad construct. It may refer to the physical, social, organizational, cultural, or psychological properties of a college or university. Baird, in his thorough review of the literature on college environments, suggests that they may be studied in four ways: demographically, perceptually, behaviorally, and through a combination of the preceding three methods.

For the purposes of this review, the aspect of the environment that appears to have been most important in understanding the link between what the college offers and student responsibility is the psychological feel or climate of the campus. This psychological dimension typically has been addressed as a perceptual phenomena and has been studied through student and faculty responses to questionnaire items. That is, the institution is crucial in accounting for student outcomes. One important advantage of regarding the college environment as a perceptual phenomena, amenable to paper and pencil questionnaire-type descriptions, is that the resulting quantitative descriptions are incorporated readily into the regression and causal modeling approaches that we have previously reviewed.

The aspect of the perceptual environment that we will examine is the students' perceptions that they "fit" into the college environment. If students' goals can be realized, then the environment is generally supportive of their development. This sense of fit, belonging, or integration is an important element in affecting the quality of students' efforts and shapes the extent and nature of students' encounters with faculty and peers.

Institutional and Individual Fit
The concept of "fit" has a long history in psychology. One line of research concerning the impact of the college envi-

ronment on student behavior and ultimately college outcomes follows from Tinto's use of the "fit" construct in the college context. Citing Rootman (1972), Tinto argues that voluntary withdrawal from college can be seen as the cumulative strain produced by a lack of "person-role" fit between the student and the normative academic and social expectations of the institution. This cumulative strain erodes an individual's commitment and loyalty to the college and ultimately leads to withdrawal.

Typical of this work is a study by Pascarella and Chapman (1983), who conducted a multi-institutional path analytic study of student persistence. Their findings affirm the centrality of institutional commitment on persistence at four-year commuter and residential institutions and at two-year colleges. Of interest was their finding that at the residential four-year schools, institutional loyalty was largely affected by a student's social integration, while at the commuter campuses, commitment was influenced primarily by academic integration.

As a follow-up to the differential findings for commuter and residential institutions, Pascarella, Duby, and Iverson (1983) conducted a longitudinal path analytic study of 269 freshmen enrolled at a large urban, commuter, doctoral institution. Their findings confirm the role that academic integration plays in shaping institutional commitment. However, in this single-institution study, institutional commitment did not have a significant effect on persistence decisions at the end of the freshman year. These findings again were confirmed by Glover (1992) who, using a data set based on responses to Pace's CSEQ, implemented Tinto's model of persistence at six commuter institutions. Using causal modeling techniques, she found that the only significant contributor to institutional commitment was the degree of student academic integration. Unlike Pascarella, Duby, and Iverson (1983), Glover found that commitment significantly affected students' self-reported gains in general education, although to a much lesser extent than did academic integration. Terenzini and Wright (1987), using an abridged version of Tinto's model, also report that the impact of academic integration is a crucial feature in retention.

Another line of research developed separately from that of Tinto but consistent with his thinking was advanced by John Bean (1980). Bean's thinking was informed by studies of turnover in the workplace. At that time Bean, using causal modeling and data collected at a major Midwestern university with more than 1,000 freshmen, defined a variable termed "institutional commitment." Specifically, Bean described it as "the degree of loyalty toward membership in an organization." Results of the analysis indicated that for both men and women, institutional commitment was the single most important variable in accounting for persistence.

In an attempt to untangle the interrelationship between students' performance in college and their satisfaction with college, Bean and Bradley conducted a secondary analysis of student data collected at a single institution (1986). One of the key variables in the model was institutional fit, which was defined by a series of items tapping a student's sense of belonging at the university. They found that satisfaction with being a student had a greater influence on performance (GPA) than did performance on satisfaction. That is, GPA did not have as great an influence on satisfaction as satisfaction did on GPA. Institutional fit was found to be the single most important predictor of satisfaction for women and the third best predictor for men. Thus college loyalty is related to the satisfaction that students derive from being students, and this, in turn, affects performance.

While the work of Tinto and Bean are complementary, it remained for Cabrera et al. to demonstrate the empirical convergence of these two approaches (1992). Of interest to us is their examination of Tinto's institutional-commitment construct and Bean's institutional-fit construct. Using causal modeling methodology and data derived from traditional-aged students at a single institution, they tested the efficacy of each construct separately and then the overlap between the two in a third analysis. They report a strong correlation between the two constructs ($r = .79$), and a model that examined the equality of the constructs proved highly satisfactory.

Pace has provided an important perspective in understanding the role of fit between the individual and the campus (1984). He suggests that students who perceive their environment to be friendly, congenial, open, accessible, and supportive are more likely to be satisfied with their experience than students who sense that the campus community is closed to them. Further, Pace suggests that when congruency or person-environment fit exists, students are more likely to achieve their academic and social objectives for coming to college.

Pace has expressed his views about the environment in the form of rating scales which are part of the CSEQ (1984). Two major constructs are defined: the relational environment, which includes a student's perception of the accessibility of faculty and administrators and the friendliness of other students, and the mission or purpose of the college, either scholarly, aesthetically, or vocationally oriented. These two aspects of the environment (relational and mission) constitute the ethos of the campus, and individuals who fit the emphasis of a campus are more likely to be supported in their learning and development.

As part of the normative study of the CSEQ, Pace reports on the relative contribution perception of the environment makes in predicting self-reported student gains in a large, multi-institutional data set (1982). Across four types of gains, student perception of environment makes a small but significant contribution. In each regression analysis, environment measure accounted for a small proportion of the variation in the gain measure. Of course, the largest single contributor was the quality of effort students put into their work. Pace reports an analysis of the environment scales by institutional type in the CSEQ manual (1984). Liberal arts institutions are more likely than either doctoral universities or public, comprehensive colleges to report large proportions of students who perceive the climate as accessible and supportive of scholarly and intellectual activities. The public, comprehensive institutions and the less selective, general liberal arts colleges are more likely to emphasize vocational competence for their students.

In a study of student quality of effort and institutional environment at six selected metropolitan universities, Arnold et al., using multiple regression, found that a positive interpersonal climate contributed in a small but significant way to student gains in personal development, general education, and vocational preparation (1991). The perceived emphasis on scholarly activities contributed to gains in all areas other than vocational preparedness. The perceived emphasis on vocational skills contributed most heavily to self-reported gains in vocational preparation. An effort by Mencke, Sahoo, and Kroc, using causal modeling procedures in a pilot study of retention at a large doctoral institution, found that Pace's relational environment items, drawn from the CSEQ, were positively related to student involvement for male students (1988).

In a study to apply and develop Pace's general model of student outcomes, Davis and Murrell (1993) employed causal modeling procedures on a large sample of students drawn from Kuh et. al.'s "Involving Colleges" study (1991). Like Arnold et. al., this study was not designed to examine the effects of institutional demographics (size, type, percent residential) on students' perceptions of the environment. Rather, it examined the manner in which student background, perceived institutional climate, and student effort interacted to affect student gains. They found that the perceived institutional environment exerted an important shaping effect on all the model's components. They concluded that a facilitative environment favorably shapes perceptions of other aspects of the institution's mission (scholarly and vocational) and facilitates student responsibility as well. A supportive environment had a direct and indirect impact on learning, development, and vocational preparedness. Environment led to important direct effects on students' academic and social effort. Effort, in turn, was the most important contributor to self-reported outcomes.

Qualitative Approaches

Before closing this section on college environment, we need to join with others (Tinto 1987; Terenzini and Pascarella 1990; Pascarella 1991) in welcoming qualitative studies of how students from various backgrounds perceive the college environment and, in turn, work to achieve their collegiate goals. Over the last 10 years and especially the last five, some excellent descriptions of colleges as cultural entities have been written. No doubt this approach will continue to bear fruit in the future (Horowitz 1987; Kuh and Whitt 1988; Masland 1985; Moffatt 1991). These descriptions provide much texture and offer rich, often powerful, images of the college experience. Two such qualitative studies offer important examples of the way in which qualitative approaches, informed by theories of college outcomes, can enrich our understanding of the collegiate experience for students.

George Kuh and his associates present the results of hundreds of interviews with students, faculty, and campus administrators at 14 diverse institutions nominated as "Involving Colleges" (1991). Their perspective was informed by the work of Pace, Astin, Pascarella, and Tinto. The findings emphasize the importance of focusing on creating distinctive institutional contexts that emphasize the importance of student responsibility and initiative.

A narrower but more focused study of the influence of student perceptions on social integration sought to test Tinto's model of student departure. Christie and Dinham interviewed 25 full-time freshman students at a single large research university (1991). Of those 25 students, four withdrew from college. The findings, following Tinto, confirmed the importance of social integration in retention decisions. Of note, however, was the importance of external influences on students' ability to become integrated. The findings highlight the importance of high school friends and family in limiting time spent on campus and thus interfering with the ability of students to fit in and make the transition to college life. This alienation from a college circle may contribute to a sense of social isolation and thus erode a student's commitment to complete coursework. Clearly, this study is consistent with previous quantitative research and forces us to think deeply about the importance of noncollegiate influences on degree completion.

It would be easy to believe that our lack of success lies not in ourselves but in our environment— that is, our organizations, leaders, or society.

Summary and Retrospective

In concluding this section, it is appropriate to look back and reflect on what has passed. The college environment can be understood to consist of two components: the first defined by the formal demographic features of the institution and the second by the individual student's sense of belonging or fit within the institution. The demographic features, especially large institutional size and commuter context, exert a small but inhibitory effect on student outcomes. The absence of smaller-scale spaces, either psychological or physical, may contribute to a sense of anomie in which the individual can find no like-minded comrades with whom to share the college passage. The latter, psychological feel of the campus, especially the sense of a good fit between the school and the individual, can facilitate positive student outcomes such as persistence and can promote a climate in which students are willing to involve themselves in their academic work.

It would be easy to believe that our lack of success lies not in ourselves but in our environment—that is, our organizations, leaders, or society. The good news for campus *administrators* is that research suggests campus environment can be a source of strength for learners if small-scale, human environments—supportive of learning and learners—are created. The good news for *students* is that they can achieve their personal and academic goals if they take some responsibility. The most important factor that affects student learning is *what the student does.* The environment may shape or press an individual, but it does not determine college outcomes. Determination of college outcomes lies with faculty and administrators but, most of all, with students.

COLLEGE OUTCOMES

*What battle was ever won without an effort? What great
act achieved without resolution?*
Helme

In the preceding sections we have examined the contribution
that individual student characteristics make to the outcomes
of college, and we have reviewed the effect of the college
environment upon students. As a broad generality, what students bring to college in the form of their background is relatively unimportant in determining what they take from the
experience. In the case of gender, it does affect the way in
which they relate to the academic and social life of the campus.

The formal features of the college environment—especially
large sized, as we have seen—can exert a small but negative
impact on a student's sense of belonging and thus inhibit
involvement. Of some importance is the degree to which students perceive they fit in. That sense of connectedness or
community may serve to promote satisfactory collegiate outcomes such as retention, personal development, and intellectual gains. While the role of the collegiate environment
appears to be more significant than student background in
promoting college outcomes, neither exerts a decisive effect.
As we will see in the next section, the factor that is overrid-
ingly important in understanding why students do well or
poorly in college is the extent to which they invest themselves
in their college work.

Tinto and Pascarella: Integration and Interaction
In this section we will approach the review of the evidence
of the effect of student responsibility on positive college outcomes from the perspective of the major contributors to this
conversation. The perspective of Tinto has been investigated
by Pascarella and his colleagues and students. Pascarella's
emphasis on the importance of student-faculty and student-
peer interactions on college outcomes has grown from Tinto's
academic and social integration constructs. For this reason,
we will examine the research which followed from both of
these theoretical approaches as a single body.

Tinto makes a sharp distinction between academic and
social integration (1975). He defines students' academic integration as the congruence of development and intellectual
expectations with the normative standards of the institution.
Social integration is a congruence between an individual's

expectations for peer and faculty contact and support and an institution's standards for such support. Tinto notes that social interactions, especially those with faculty, are likely to promote academic integration. Thus, a student's interactions with students and peers can either encourage or discourage academic work. For Pascarella, the importance of student-faculty and student-peer interaction lies in the fact that these interactions can orient students to expected behavior at college. This, in turn, will promote or discourage the level of student effort and perhaps directly affect student outcomes as well. As these two complementary perspectives share a common research base, we will examine that base as a single body.

We have tabled selected research studies that deal with the role of student integration and student-faculty and student-peer interaction. The studies were chosen for several reasons. Some were selected because they represent significant, ground-breaking efforts. Most were selected because they featured strong methodologies; others because they represented interesting findings or suggested new directions. We have focused on the most important findings and tabled only the most robust effects reported in the studies.

Table 1 lists a consistent series of studies that emphasize the importance of academic and social integration and interaction with faculty and peers in college outcomes. Closer examination suggests six other interesting findings which have implications for our understanding of the sometimes-complex way in which student integration is tied to college outcomes as well as conducting future research in this area.

TABLE 1
Summary of Findings for Student Integration

Study & Date	Sample	Analysis	Principal Findings Independent Variables on Outcome Variables
Pascarella and Terenzini (1977)	One university freshman	Regression and discriminant	Student-faculty informal interaction on retention
Terenzini and Pascarella (1977)	One university freshman	MANOVA and discriminant	Academic and social integration on persistence

TABLE 1 (continued)

Summary of Findings for Student Integration

Study & Date	Sample	Analysis	Principal Findings Independent Variables on Outcome Variables
Terenzini and Pascarella (1980)	One university freshman	Regression	1) SAT and faculty discussion on academic performance 2) Faculty discussion on intellectual development 3) Peer interaction on personal development
Pascarella and Terenzini (1980)	One university freshman	MCOVA and discriminant	Student-faculty relations on persistence
Munro (1981)	National NLS-72 longitudinal	Path analysis	Academic integration on persistence and institutional commitment
Endo and Harpel (1982)	One university four year longitudinal	Path analysis	Frequency of formal and informal faculty contact on personal, intellectual outcomes and satisfaction but not on grades
Pascarella, Duby, Iverson (1983)	One university freshman commuters	Path analysis	Academic integration on persistence
Pascarella and Terenzini (1983)	One university freshman residential	Path analysis	1) Academic and social integration on commitment & persistence

TABLE 1 (continued)
Summary of Findings for Student Integration

Study & Date	Sample	Analysis	Principal Findings Independent Variables on Outcome Variables
Pascarella and Chapman (1983)	Commuter and residential two and four year institutions freshman	Path analysis	1) Academic and social integration on institutional commitment and degree commitment 2) Institutional and degree commitment on persistence 3) Social integration key for residential 4) Academic integration key for commuter
Terenzini, Theophilides, and Lorang (1984)	One selective university three year longitudinal	Regression	Classroom involvement in academic skill development
Weidman (1985)	One urban university low SES, female	Interviews	Social integration important in minority persistence
Volkwein, King, and Terenzini (1986)	One university transfer students	Regression	1) Classroom involvement on intellectual skill development 2) Quality student-faculty contact on academic content
Hearn (1987)	Two universities	Path analysis	Academic performance on aspirations for graduate study
Stoecker, Pascarella, and Wolfle (1988)	National CIRP data longitudinal	Path analysis	Academic and social integration on persistence

TABLE 1 (continued)

Summary of Findings for Student Integration

Study & Date	Sample	Analysis	Principal Findings Independent Variables on Outcome Variables
Walleri and Peglow-Hoch (1988)	One community college poorly prepared students	Interviews	1) Faculty contact key in persistence 2) Peer contact important in persistence
Glover (1992)	Six commuter urban universities	Causal modeling	1) Academic integration on institutional and degree commitment 2) Gain in general education
Mutter (1992)	One large urban community college	Regression	1) Institutional commitment on persistence 2) Academic integration on persistence 3) Social integration of minimal influence on persistence

First, we see in Table 1 a remarkably long, theoretically informed string of studies on the factors associated with student withdrawal. Over the last 15 years, our understanding of the role of student integration in a variety of settings with different student groups and different outcome measures has left us with a solid understanding of the importance of developing academic programs and practices which promote student integration.

Second, as we scan down the column marked "Sample," we are struck by the progression from single-institution studies with limited generalizability to multi-institutional, comparative studies to those that make use of national data bases (CIRP, NLS-72). Thus, the state of the art in this field of study really places a premium on multi-institutional studies. Exceptions to this, however, are those studies that break ground by attempting to test our generalities with different groups

---

of individuals or with little-studied institutional types, such as the community college. For these, early studies may profit from initial single-institution, "descriptive" studies, although we anticipate that stronger work will need to make use of national data sets. And most recently, a set of studies examined the role of student integration in the community college setting and the status of underrepresented groups.

Third, as with study samples, we observe some interesting developments in methodology. Early studies made use of regression and analysis of variance (ANOVA) designs. Methodologically, the state-of-the-art studies in this field now regularly make use of path models or structural-equation models as a means of exploring the direct and indirect effects of theoretically derived variables on one another and on college outcomes. Of special interest is the recent use of qualitative, interview-based studies. These may provide scholars and practitioners with a richly textured vision of how students grow and learn.

Finally, in the column titled "Principal Findings," we are struck with the consistency of the evidence that student-faculty interaction and academic integration exert a direct and important effect on persistence, intellectual and academic outcomes, and institutional loyalty. Peer relations appear to be important in enhancing persistence and personal development. These findings appear especially strong in commuter settings and the community college. Social integration appears to play its strongest role in the residential institution, and the evidence for its contribution in the commuter setting is mixed. Of course, these studies tell us about issues in current practice. Indeed, there is very little evidence regarding the role that social integration might play in commuter settings if a concerted effort was made to socially involve commuters and move them to active learning with peers and faculty. The existing studies describe how things are, not how they might become.

Astin and Student Involvement

The best single source of evidence concerning the importance of student involvement in promoting positive collegiate outcomes comes from Astin's own massive analysis of the national CIRP data set (1993). For Astin, student involvement is a broad but simple concept. Initially, he defined student involvement as the "amount of physical and psychological

energy that the student devotes to the academic experience" (1984, p. 297). More recently, Astin has expanded this concept of involvement to include a range of practices that bring a student and college together. In his book *What Matters in College*, Astin applies his I-E-O model (input, environment, output) to the analysis of the longitudinal records of more than 24,000 students enrolled at literally hundreds of institutions nationwide. For Astin, student involvement is an aspect of the environment, along with institutional practices, faculties, and peers. In his model using multiple regression analysis, he accounts for student "input" characteristics first and then assesses the contribution that various student-involvement behaviors make to college outcomes. Some of the measures of involvement that are assessed include hours spent studying, participation in various programs, and contact with peers. Clearly, there is much conceptual overlap between Astin's student-involvement theory and Tinto's concept of student integration. Pascarella, in promoting the importance of faculty and student-peer interaction, also provides a theoretical link (1985).

While Astin's analysis is far-ranging, there are three areas of student involvement that are especially important for our purposes: involvement with other students, with faculty, and with work (1993). When students report close, personal relationships with one or more faculty members, exemplified by the student as being a guest in a professor's home, assisting in teaching, or working on a research project with a faculty member, for example, a wide variety of positive outcomes follow. Student-faculty contact is correlated with student satisfaction, college GPA, graduation, and enrollment in graduate school. Such interaction, even after controlling for most individual student differences, is positively associated with intellectual and personal growth.

As with student-faculty involvement, the involvement of students with one another around social and academic topics promotes a wide range of positive outcomes, even after controlling for many individual and institutional differences. When students help one another on class projects, discuss assignments, participate in social organizations, or simply socialize with different kinds of people, good things follow. Students who are socially involved also make gains in general knowledge and intellectual skills and tend to be more satisfied with their college experience. Of special interest is the finding that peer tutoring is strongly correlated with academic outcomes, including GRE scores.

There are some kinds of involvement, especially those which take students away from their studies or isolate them from the campus environment, that appear to have a negative effect on college outcomes. Astin reports that the single largest negative effect on degree completion is holding a full-time or a part-time job off campus (1993). Working has a negative effect on other outcomes too, such as GPA, growth in cultural awareness, college satisfaction, and willingness to re-enroll in college. The effects are apparent even after controlling for individual and institutional differences. Student commuting produces nearly the same strongly negative effects as holding a job off campus. These factors, prevalent at today's metropolitan universities, work to undermine the very goals for which students strive in attending college. Evidently, when compared with students without external obligations, employment off campus and commuting to campus diminish the frequency and strength of a student's involvement with faculty and peers. One is left to wonder if institutions do their students a service by promoting themselves as accessible without also clearly indicating that student obligations for involvement extend beyond mere appearances in classes.

Pace and the Quality of Student Effort

We have previously described Pace's theory of college impress. The theory's central feature, which accounts for college student learning and development, is the quality of effort that students invest in their college experience. This includes taking advantage of the physical accommodations that the college offers as well as participating in the academic and social life of the institution. The extent to which a student invests high quality of effort is marked by the time and depth of commitment a student gives to the college experience (Pace 1982). Indeed, a unique feature of Pace's questionnaire is the assumption that all of the activities measured are voluntary. Each act presumes some initiative on the part of the student. This feature makes the concept of quality of effort and the CSEQ especially appropriate to our understanding of student responsibility.

Pace's definition of effort is clearly comparable to Astin's definition of involvement as the investment of "physical and psychological energy" (1984). Pace's operationalization of quality of effort, through the 14 scales of the CSEQ, encompasses Tinto's academic and social integration construct as well as Pascarella's specification of effort and student-faculty and peer interaction. In this overlap between the theories of Tinto, Pascarella, Astin, and Pace, we see a broader and unifying construct which is students' responsibility for their own learning. What makes Pace's contribution unique is his thorough description of what constitutes responsible student behavior.

As discussed previously, Appendix 1 contains a description of the 14 quality of effort scales which collectively describe what is meant by student responsibility.

Unfortunately, as Pascarella and Terenzini note, relatively few published studies have utilized the CSEQ in studying the manner in which student effort works to achieve student learning and development (1991). The fullest use of the CSEQ and the concept of quality of effort has been made by hundreds of colleges across the country. These institutions' purposes and findings have largely been directed at resolving local problems. For example, Pace describes the use of the CSEQ at four separate colleges and universities as a tool in accreditation self-study processes (1988). Other uses include special studies for particular local groups; use as a tool in improving student retention and the quality of student life; facilitating discussion on campuses about teaching and learning; and as a contributing element in institutional renewal. Another example of local use was presented by Pace in a symposium convened at the 1992 meeting of the Association for the Study of Higher Education. The symposium featured four longitudinal studies completed at different institutions. Each of the four institutions made use of the CSEQ in a test-retest situation for distinctly local purposes.

A unique feature of Pace's questionnaire is the assumption that all of the activites measured are voluntary.

An example of a single institutional application of the CSEQ is provided by Flannelly in which two freshman and senior classes at the University of North Carolina were surveyed using the CSEQ for the purpose of describing "student progress here at the university" (1990). Their findings suggested that high levels of student-faculty contact coincided with strong student quality of effort, and that student achievement and development appeared to follow from high levels of student effort.

We believe that a sizeable, fugitive literature regarding student effort has been accumulated by individual institutions.

Unlike the instrumentation that was developed to examine the theoretical constructs of Tinto and Pascarella or the elegant secondary analysis completed by Astin of CIRP data, Pace's CSEQ has largely been used for practical purposes. Perhaps one of the reasons the CSEQ has been so widely used is that the content of the instrument is so obviously related to learning and student development.

Of the several published studies which do make use of the CSEQ, two are single-institution inquiries that fail to control for individual differences. Stone and Strange administered the CSEQ to a sample of 238 student athletes at a single, large, NCAA Division 1-A institution (1989). They found that gender was substantially unrelated to the quality of effort of student athletes. In fact, the athlete group differed in only small ways from a nonathlete comparison group. In another single institutional study, Ory and Braskamp used the CSEQ to describe students enrolled in two special academic programs and to compare them with students enrolled in the regular curriculum (1988). The two special programs were an honors program and a "transition" program designed for disadvantaged students.

Using one-way ANOVA and pairwise correlation procedures, the researchers concluded that the honors group showed a greater level of effort than the other groups and reported making greater academic and personal/social gains. Noteworthy was the finding that both special program groups (honors and transition) "appeared to get more for their effort than did the regular students" (p. 128). They conclude that the distinctive environment and unique opportunities for learning of these two special programs may have led to stronger active participation in the college experience and thus greater self-reported gains.

Two studies which do make use of multi-institutional data sets and multivariate analytical procedures are those offered by Arnold et al. (1991) and Davis and Murrell (1993). Each of these studies has made use of the CSEQ data base maintained by Pace at UCLA's Center for the Study of Evaluation. Both studies focused on institutions with specific characteristics. The former study included six metropolitan universities, and the latter 11 "involving institutions." For both studies, a portion of the data was gathered under the auspices of the College Experiences Study by Kuh et al. (1991).

Arnold et al. (1991), using multiple regression analysis,

included both individual student background characteristics and perceptions of the collegiate environment along with four measures of student effort to predict a variety of college gains. The 14 quality of effort scales were reduced to four additive-effort factors. These factors were titled *academic effort, interpersonal effort, use of group facilities,* and *effort in science.* Of the statistically significant relationships, those with the largest standardized beta weights for each gain measure included:

- Interpersonal effort and facilities-use affected gains in personal development;
- Effort in science and affected gains in science and technology;
- Interpersonal and academic-effort affected gains in general education;
- Effort in science and academics affected gains in intellectual skills; and
- The vocational environment of the institution and academic-effort affected gains in vocational preparation.

While institutional environment and the interaction effects of student age and enrollment status also were significant, their contribution to gains was relatively slight. Clearly, these results suggest that, for new majority students enrolled in metropolitan universities, the strongest contributor to student outcomes is the effort that students put into their own studies.

Findings reported by Davis and Murrell are consistent with those described above (1993). Using causal modeling procedures that allowed for the identification of direct and indirect effects, a model of student outcomes was built on the basis of Pace's general theory.

Controlling for student variables including sex, age, and family background, the researchers found that academic effort made the strongest contribution to gains in general education. Social effort made the strongest contribution to gains in personal and social development, and academic effort and a generally supportive relational environment made the strongest contributions to gains in vocational preparedness.

While these two studies strongly support Pace's proposition that the quality of a student's effort is the most important factor in accounting for student outcomes, they are limited in that the institutional samples used reflect only certain kinds of colleges. Three of the most comprehensive studies of the impact of quality of effort on student outcomes were completed by Pace, making use of the CSEQ data base accumulated at UCLA (1982; 1984; 1990). In these studies, Pace used the normative data gathered in the process of instrument development and the subsequent accumulated data from colleges and universities who used the CSEQ.

Pace reports the results of two separate multiple-regression analyses of CSEQ data (1982; 1984). The results of the first analysis of data collected in 1979 at 11 varied colleges and the second, conducted on data collected at eight additional institutions, are quite consistent. When student background, status, environment, and, finally, quality of effort variables were entered into the regression model in order, both analyses showed that the effort scales make a large contribution in accounting for student gains. This was true even after controlling for student background, status, and environment. Effort was strongly related to gains in personal development, general education, and science, and moderately so for gains in general intellectual skills and vocational preparedness. Generally, these findings proved to be consistent with subsequent research which made use of the CSEQ.

In the book *The Undergraduates*, Pace makes use of a "breadth index," a construct which has great promise for theory-testing research conducted with the CSEQ (1990). The breadth index represents by a single figure the extent of a student's college effort across all of the CSEQ's quality of effort scales. Breadth of effort has been defined as the "number of areas of college experience in which a student's quality of effort score is above average" (p. 115). As many students are nonresidential, if we exclude the scale that taps residency there are 13 quality of effort scales. A student who produces an above-average level of effort in 10 of the 13 scales would have a breadth score of 10. Similarly, a student who is involved in only three areas would have a breadth index of three. Now, it happens that not all students excel in all areas, nor do most students fail to exert effort in at least one or two areas. The distribution of breadth scores reported by Pace for more than 10,000 students enrolled at 33 various colleges is approximately normal.

This concept of "breadth" captures the spirit of the college experience perhaps better than any other aggregate measure of effort. In analyzing the impact of breadth of effort on college gains, Pace presents a table that compares students with low breadth scores (0-3) with those who have high breadth scores (9-13). In general, students with limited involvement across a range of areas report markedly lower gains across all areas academic, social, and vocational. Another analysis compares students with high and low breadth scores on college satisfaction. The differences between the two groups is vast. Of those with the highest breadth scores, more than 60 percent report being very satisfied with their college experience, while more than 30 percent of the students with the most limited breadth scores report being very or somewhat dissatisfied with their college experience.

One of the features of the CSEQ that makes it a rich and powerful instrument for local institutional improvement efforts is the range and detail of the data that are provided by each of the 14 quality of effort scales. However, for theory-testing purposes, especially for regression and path analytic modeling, the sheer number of scales can be potentially distracting from the central message of Pace's work. What is needed is an integrative measure of a student's level of effort that can be used with other data provided, perhaps, by the CSEQ or mixed with data from other sources. For work of this kind, the breadth index should be a measure of choice.

Summary

We see a marked similarity in the findings that have been derived from the work of Tinto, Pascarella, Astin, and Pace. We are reminded of Pascarella and Terenzini's observation that there is "a certain wholeness to the college experience" (1991, p. 626). That wholeness is found in the balance of social and academic work that students who make positive gains in college appear to experience. The totality of the college experience includes classwork, important mentoring relations with faculty, and a peer group that shares and promotes the intellectual adventure that is college. Students who take the responsibility to invest themselves in this experience are rewarded. Institutions that promise students a college experience for merely the price of tuition are making promises they cannot keep.

Retrospective: Enhancing the College Experience

The body of research we have reviewed represents one of the strongest and sustained accounts about what it takes to succeed in college. It speaks to students and those charged with guiding our nation's colleges and universities. We know what is needed to enhance the college experience.

In this review, we have discussed the contributions of four theorists. Each has provided a special perspective on the essentials as well as the details of college success. Robert Pace offers "college impress" and the quality of student effort. Vincent Tinto's ground-breaking synthesis points us to student integration, both academic and social, as the driving force behind satisfactory college outcomes. Ernest Pascarella has given us a theoretically elegant model that allows us to examine the impact of college, in general, and student-faculty and student-peer relations, in particular, on college outcomes. Finally, Alexander Astin has shown how involvement is the key to developing student talent. We take the collective offerings of these theorists as a call for student responsibility and an institutional obligation to develop practices that require and promote student involvement in the college experience.

We have tracked the methodological development of the state of the art in this field. This base reflects the careful accumulation of knowledge collectively nurtured by literally hundreds of people over a half-century of time. The research base is built around theoretically informed, strong national and multi-institutional studies that take advantage of multivariate statistical procedures. These techniques assist us in establishing the generality of the findings as well as accounting for individual student and institutional differences.

We know that the effects of initial, individual student differences on college outcomes are relatively slight and are largely mediated by the manner in which the student engages the college experience. In general, we are struck by the similarities—rather than the differences—between student groups in the manner in which student effort and institutional context play out in affecting college outcomes.

The college context has two elements: the structural features of the organization (size, type, character) and the climate or "ethos." Generally, structural features that tend to isolate students and promote an ethos of anonymity produce poor college outcomes. College climates that are characterized by a strong sense of direction and care and those that build student involvement tend to promote favorable outcomes directly and indirectly by promoting student-faculty and student-peer relations as well as establishing an expectation that students will behave responsibly. Finally, the decisive single factor in affecting college outcomes is the degree to which students are integrated into the life of the campus, interact with faculty and peers, and become involved in their studies.

In the next section we will examine some initiatives in college programs and practices which respond to the directions indicated by the research literature.

Implications of Student Responsibility

Responsibility's like a string we can only see the middle of.
Both ends are out of sight.
William McFee

In dreams begin responsibilities.
Delmore Schwartz

The concept of student responsibility can serve as a central
vision for understanding and enhancing teaching and learning
on college campuses. In this final section we will explore
some of the implications of this concept for researchers as
well as for administrators, faculty, and students.

Implications for Inquiry

We have seen in these pages the development of an idea. The
concept of student responsibility and its manifestation in student behavior, as central to the educational process, has
evolved slowly over the last 25 years. Through this time, our
understanding of what makes for a successful collegiate experience has been informed increasingly by theory. Indeed,
theory-guided research in higher education is the key to
advancing our understanding of this complex and changing
field. It is only in retrospect that we can fully grasp the importance of deliberate theory testing and systematic research
informed by theory. What we now take as a strong body of
common knowledge must have looked far less certain and
incomplete to those beginning college outcomes studies of
the late 1970s.

Our institutions are complex, our students are diverse, and
the number of contributing factors to college outcomes is
great. Studies in our field must rely on large, multi-
institutional data sets and multivariate statistical approaches
if we are to manage the difficulties attendant to "valid" and
"generalizable" knowledge. The day is long past when simple
bivariate correlation or ANOVA designs will allow us to
advance our understanding in this field of study. We must continue to develop theory that will guide our knowledge of
higher education through time.

One's selection of variables reflects a vision of what is
important in determining student outcomes. It is our belief
that human development and academic achievement in college can be satisfactorily accounted for if the social context
and students' ability and willingness to invest in their own

education are included in our calculations. A limiting and superficial focus on the impact of classificatory variables on outcome, without accounting for individual effort, social context, or the complex process by which development occurs, impoverishes the research act and our understanding of the way human beings learn and develop.

Further work is needed which extends the principles of student responsibility to groups of students that have not been fully represented in past studies. We believe that subsequent research will confirm the general importance of what students themselves do in accounting for collegiate outcomes. We see issues of student diversity as going beyond demographics to include individual differences in learning preferences, ability, and behavior as well as the interaction effects of the environment with these individual characteristics. We believe that there is a strong need for research which accounts for other influences on college outcomes including institutional practices, governance, culture, and context. The inclusion of variables such as campus culture, governance arrangements, leadership style, and institutional type will enrich our understanding of the way in which student responsibility can be shaped by our practices.

Finally, we offer a reminder that the quantitative paradigm has served us well in the advancement of our knowledge of institutional effect on student development. Through large, multi-institutional studies, using procedures that are replicable, we have been able to produce findings that are testable and generalizable. Recently developed, sophisticated statistical methodology and computer capability have enabled us to analyze data sets that previously would have been unwieldy. The theory that has resulted from this work has provided a rational and empirical model to support our intuitive sense of how student development occurs.

Other methods that build on and augment this existing knowledge also will serve our collective enterprise. Narrative-based approaches, used mindfully of what has occurred in the past, are necessary to tease out the nuances and discern the subtleties that permeate the wide range of individual differences found in today's college students. It is hoped that these two methodologies will complement each other to give us a more complete and accurate picture of the complex process of the growth of students as they move through our institutions. The interplay of qualitative and quantitative studies should enrich our understanding and give shading and texture to the mosaic that is our student.

Implications for Practice

In this report we have offered a definition of student responsibility by describing what students should do to fully take advantage of what college has to offer. We have examined the context or web of elements that shape students' responsibility and thus college outcomes. Now is the time to consider recommendations for institutional action that center around developing and sustaining responsible student involvement in college life. In truth, we approach this task with considerable humility. Over the past decade there has been a steady stream of recommendations for institutional policy and practice that has centered around issues of student involvement, integration, active learning, student diversity, student effort, and responsibility.

The first initiative is best reflected in the "active learning" approach and suggests a set of pedagogical activities that maximize student involvement.

The early 1980s saw a growing concern for the effectiveness of American higher education. This concern initially found expression in a U.S. Department of Education report authored by several of the most respected figures in the field. In 1984, the National Institute of Education (NIE) study group, under the chairmanship of Kenneth Mortimer, issued its *Involvement in Learning* report. Ten years ago the group warned that "the realities of student learning, curricular coherence, the quality of facilities, faculty morale, and academic standards no longer measure up to our expectations" (p. 8). We echo the report's central critique of our institutions' "temptation toward generating the maximum number of student credit hours without regard to the quality of learning" (p. 12). A major conclusion was that for learning to be of any quality, students must become actively engaged in the process. Among the report's many specific recommendations were two key reforms designed to enhance student involvement:

Faculty should make greater use of active modes of teaching and require that students take greater responsibility for their learning (p. 27)

and

Every institution of higher education should strive to create learning communities, organized around specific intellectual themes or tasks (p. 33).

Rather than offer yet another set of recommendations, it better suits the purpose of this review to revisit these two established approaches for reform of higher education. The first initiative is best reflected in the "active learning" approach and suggests a set of *pedagogical* activities that maximize student involvement in learning with other students. The other is the "learning community" model and affects the *structure* of the curriculum and the organization of delivery systems. Both of these reforms have a history and have been identified since at least the early 1980s as complementary tools with which to renew higher education. We believe they offer the greatest promise for building an environment that will nurture responsible student behavior. Taken together, they also demand a reconceptualization of the purpose of higher education and a rethinking of our role in the lives of our learners.

The NIE report argues that an overreliance on lecture approaches to teaching and learning is one of the most stultifying barriers to faculty renewal and student academic achievement. Student learning is tied to the relative engagement that learners experience with the content, and active learning means active students, not passive note-takers. Student involvement is strongly affected by teaching methods. Classroom activities that require active discussion, topical assignments, problem solving, in-class presentations, and student participation in decisions about content and activities all promote a sense of responsible involvement. Approaches such as peer tutoring push students to sharpen their competence and to view themselves as responsible. Building connections between course content and students' lives is essential, and integrating out-of-class, "real world" elements into the curriculum can help to bring the two into closer harmony.

Bonwell and Eison (1991) provide some helpful characteristics of active learning:

1. Students are involved in more than listening.
2. Less emphasis is placed on transmitting information and more on developing students' skills.
3. Students are involved in higher-order thinking (analysis, synthesis, evaluation).
4. Students are engaged in activities such as reading, discussing, and writing).
5. Greater emphasis is placed on students' exploration of their own attitudes and values (p. 2).

Even very traditional activities such as note-taking can engage learners if teachers make an effort to teach paraphrasing, summarizing, and questioning techniques. The level of involvement in a discussion can be influenced by the types of questions the instructor asks as well as his or her skill at pushing for higher-order thinking. Certainly the methods of assessment a teacher chooses and the kinds of tests used can influence the degree to which students either grapple with the meaning of the material or simply regurgitate facts.

One approach is cooperative learning, a set of learning strategies in which students working in pairs or small teams complete structured activities in a collaborative rather than competitive manner. To be successful, such efforts must be carefully structured and followed by the instructor to ensure that all students are actively engaged in the task and are exercising appropriate problem-solving skills. These approaches may be used within the context of a relatively brief 15- or 20-minute exercise designed to review past material or to set the stage for the introduction of new material. Alternatively, this approach might be applied to a complex multiclass task that could stretch over several weeks. The ASHE-ERIC Higher Education Report titled *Cooperative Learning: Increasing College Faculty Instructional Productivity* (Johnson, Johnson, and Smith 1991) is an excellent guide to teachers interested in incorporating innovative approaches in their classes.

Active learning also is supported by learning models such as the Experiential Learning Model developed by David Kolb (1984). Acknowledging the diversity in learning preferences and including opportunities that connect with those differences necessitates interactive processes in addition to authoritative information-sharing. It underscores the desirability of learners' finding meaning in their experience in light of new knowledge and helps to connect the curriculum to their lives out of class. It also offers a theoretical basis for understanding the potency of collaborative and interactive classroom strategies in contributing to student development. Murrell and Claxton (1987) discuss teaching strategies, and Murrell and Davis (1992) have developed assessment and evaluation guidelines that are congruent with Kolb's model. Grading in this context becomes not a sorting process, but a learning process. It serves as a further opportunity for faculty to engage students in a deepening conversation about learning and about what matters in content mastery.

Collaborative learning approaches such as those suggested by Kenneth Bruffee (1984) serve as opportunities for students to learn interactive and interdependent behaviors, behaviors that create a sense of community and provide a vital link to responsibility. Bruffee's work has drawn many professors to try instructional methods that are more student centered. At the same time, he urges caution, saying, "Organizing collaborative learning effectively requires doing more than throwing students together with their peers with little or no guidance or preparation." To do that is merely to perpetuate, perhaps even aggravate, the many possible negative efforts of peer-group influence: conformity, anti-intellectualism, intimidation, and leveling-down of quality.

Bruffee continues, "To avoid these pitfalls ... requires us to create and maintain a demanding academic environment that makes collaboration—social engagement in intellectual pursuits—a genuine part of students' educational development." That suggests to us the need to look at the organization of our institutions as well.

The creation of learning communities responds to that need in seeking to build structural opportunities within the college which support and augment classroom-level initiatives. Learning communities are designed to build integration and create a climate of cohesion. The NIE report notes that these structures are especially important for beginning college students who may not understand the goals or methods of the academy. Since a large number of our students are first generation without role models who have attended college, they may not have a sense of their power and responsibility as learners, especially if their prior education experience has been teacher centered and authority oriented.

Learning communities help to provide students with a psychologically manageable environment. Opportunities to know the names of fellow students increase, the probability of faculty members knowing students' names increases, and the potential to know something about other members of the community is enhanced. They afford circumstances in which students' passivity and lack of participation will be visible and noticeable and thus can be challenged. The establishment of such smaller units also sends a signal to students that interaction and collaboration are important—a message that is lost if institutional practices convey the opposite.

Learning communities may assume a variety of forms, all

of which represent a real departure from the fragmentation of the curriculum that most students experience. At their most basic, they may simply reflect a link between two or more courses in which faculty members teaching each course sit in on one another's classes, and in their own classes pick up threads that emerged in the linked classes. Another form might involve the grouping of several courses around a common theme. Students take classes in a common cohort and thus have the opportunity to develop connections across content as well as among each other. Finally, the most dramatic form of learning community steps away from the typical three-credit-hour course model, presenting a curriculum organized around an academic year and within the topical area covered rebuilds course offerings of varied lengths which reflect a cross-disciplinary focus. In this case, faculty members that teach in the sequence have direct responsibility for the development of the curriculum (MacGregor et al. 1990).

Learning communities also provide ideal opportunities for collaboration between student-affairs or student-development professionals and the faculty. Residential facilities offer the most obvious venue for this to occur, but other creative approaches such as weekend classes, special lounges for adult students or ethnic groups, and electronic bulletin boards also emerge when concerned educators attack the problem of student apathy. When students see these two areas working together, it provides a model for them to emulate in reconciling their own out-of-class lives with their courses. It also helps to keep the focus of the disparate parts of the institution on a shared purpose and a desired outcome.

Whatever form they take, the major purpose of learning communities is to promote relationships. "Relationships are labs for learning to communicate, empathize, argue, and reflect" (Chickering and Reisser 1993). They enable students to make the connections between course content and their lives, to test their perspectives and perceptions against those of other students. They are especially valuable if they represent a diversity of culture and thinking, and they may be the only connecting tissue between commuting students and the institution. They help to transform the depersonalized institution into a facilitative environment where students are secure enough to process information reflectively and share those reflections, free to experience a variety of roles, to make meaningful choices, and to experience achievement (Widick,

Parker, and Knefelkamp 1978, p. 15).

Collectively, these two recommendations are designed to reshape the collegiate environment so as to promote and facilitate student involvement in and responsibility for learning. They both affect the climate or ethos of the smallest academic subunit with which students and faculty find identification. For many students, especially at large institutions, this academic unit may be "the university," and its interpersonal atmosphere exerts considerable impact on what they do and feel. Many faculty, as well, draw their greatest sense of community from their department and through it invest their intellectual and physical energy in teaching and mentoring students. Departments where faculty and students hold mutually understood values and where exchanges are frequent, friendly, and nonhierarchical likely will promote involvement. In this way the academic unit serves to reduce the psychological size of the institution and thus promotes a sense of integration and belonging which makes possible the development of individual responsibility.

The establishment of learning communities in whatever form provides ample opportunity for faculty members to explore alternative pedagogues. Indeed, new learning approaches frequently are associated with structural reforms and may be essential if such reforms are to succeed. Conversely, new pedagogues may need the support of structural changes if they are to have maximum impact. Collectively, the two aim to reshape the total institutional ethos so as to convey the sense that students must be fully engaged in learning and that the business of higher education is the student.

The foregoing recommendations have to do with institutional and faculty roles. We believe that students, too, have a role in reshaping the academy. Pascarella and Terenzini, writing in *How College Affects Students* (1991), present a compelling generalization based on their synthesis of college impact studies: "One of the most inescapable and unequivocal conclusions we can make is that the impact of college is largely determined by the individual's quality of effort and the level of involvement in both academic and nonacademic activities" (p. 610).

How can we begin to help students to understand their role as cocreators of learning? We offer four broad areas in which we believe that a dialogue between students and faculty around the issue of student responsibility should occur. First, students have the responsibility to attempt to understand themselves and their peers as learners. One of the most fundamental kinds of diversity is the difference in the way students engage with the environment. A well-educated individual should have an understanding of these differences. Faculty members need to be able to participate in this dialogue and to assist students in developing this understanding.

Second, students have a responsibility to find connections with smaller groups of individuals. At all but the smallest campuses, it is quite possible for students to become anonymous shadow figures, especially if they take no steps to overcome the forces of anonymity. The literature suggests that the antidote to isolation is to become actively involved with a "mediating subunit" on campus. Students need to find clubs, career organizations, or academic fraternities where conversations can occur that extend the discourse of the classroom. Faculty members need to encourage this activity and attest to its value.

Third, students have a responsibility to actively participate in the creation of an ethos that fosters learning. As members of the campus community, a community of scholars, it is not enough simply to show up for class. The life of a campus depends on each of the members doing his or her part to promote the ideals of the academy. Attitudes that promote a tone of disrespect and indifference or that trivialize the efforts of others to engage in the acts of knowledge creation and criticism have no place in college. A student who sits in the back of the class and sleeps helps to create a climate that ultimately tears the fabric of academic life. Teachers and students who are mutually tolerant and supportive of honest efforts toward learning contribute to an atmosphere of civility and hospitality necessary for growth and development.

Finally, students have a responsibility to become actively involved with peers and faculty in academic and cocurricular activities. Students need to ask themselves: Am I actively participating in class, not just taking notes and staring blankly into space? Am I engaged with the material, posing questions and supporting fellow students in discussion? Do I seek out faculty members? Do I make friends with peers? Do I attempt to find connections between my academic work and other aspects of my life? Faculty members who introduce these questions and assist students in realizing the value of involvement and engagement help to promote responsible student behavior.

Ideally, this conversation about learning and responsibility should begin in new-student orientation. Active learning strategies as well as learning communities help to provide a structure in which the dialogue can continue in a nonpunitive, supportive way. A mutual understanding of the faculty's role and the student's role serves to free teachers and empower learners.

This brings us to the third recommendation, the reconceptualization of our purpose. Chickering (1981) and Chickering and Reisser (1993) argue eloquently that human development is the logical choice as an overarching reason for our existence. We fully support that position. When students are brought into full partnership with faculty and staff—especially if the faculty and staff are responsibly and intentionally attending to their own growth and development—a powerful alliance is formed. Responsibility for learning feeds into a sense of competence and autonomy that is essential for functioning in a complex society. It also contributes to self-esteem and self-confidence that increase as learners experience accurate pictures of themselves and their capabilities.

Alexander Astin offered such a vision of an institution that is committed fully to student involvement as a means to student personal and intellectual growth (1985). The characteristics of such an institution would include the following:

- The entire academic community—faculty members, administrators, staff members, and students—would be united in working toward a common goal.
- Teaching and advising would be accorded a much higher priority.
- The best students would be encouraged to help in teaching the slower students.
- No more faculty stars would be lured with the promise of low or no teaching loads.
- Administrators would be hired not so much to manage as to be educational leaders.
- Students would be exposed to an environment where the values of education and of serving others took precedence over the values of acquiring resources and improving status (p. 226).

If we can agree that the above institutional picture is worth pursuing, then those of us who care about the academy must examine our own commitment to this vision. Faculty who model responsible behavior in their scholarship, their teaching, and their relationships with colleagues and their students do a great deal to promote the same behavior in their students.

The vision should be reflected unambiguously in the institutional culture, and the ethos of the campus must be one in which students feel they are members of a larger community. As student culture serves as a filter for those entering college, care must be taken to ensure that students who are inadequately prepared to invest themselves in their college studies are provided with realistic information concerning the nature of college life and what is expected to attain satisfactory academic and developmental gains. Small-scale human environments must be built in which students and faculty collectively can engage in the process of teaching and learning.

Conclusion

We conclude this report with a call for a new relationship between our institutions of higher learning and our students. During the last 25 years, our colleges have abandoned the doctrine of "in loco parentis" under which our colleges exercised parental care of students. In its place we have seen the rise of nothing short of apparent institutional indifference toward student behavior. The faculty retreat from undergraduate teaching for the rewards of research and the power of policy analysis is matched by students who appear to prefer a system that offers services for sale rather than a role in the learning process.

Our call for a new relationship is rooted in the concept of responsibility. We believe that a genuinely shared purpose among all members of the higher education community can be created on the basis of the recoupling of rights with responsibilities around issues of teaching and learning. The work of Robert Pace is a good point at which to begin thinking about the renewal of our intellectual community. As Pace reminds us, all learning is the mutual responsibility of students, faculty, and administrators.

Appendix 1

**Defining the Dimensions of Student Responsibility:
The 14 Quality of Effort Scales in the CSEQ**

Classroom (course learning scale) (10 activities)
From: relatively simple cognitive activities—such as taking notes, underlining, etc.
To: higher level cognitive activities—such as efforts to explain and organize

Library (10 activities)
From: routine, moderately exploratory use—such as using the card catalog
To: increased amount of independent exploration and focused activity—as in browsing in the stacks, developing a bibliography

Facilities related to the arts (art, music, theater scale) (12 activities)
From: attending and discussing
To: efforts toward greater understanding (seeking the views of experts and critics) and personal involvement

Facilities related to science/technology
(principles, procedures, and computers) (12 activities)
From: memorizing, watching, reading
To: efforts to explain, experiment, and develop skills

Student Union (10 activities)
From: casual and informal use—had snacks, met friends, etc.
To: programmatic use—attended events, held meetings, etc.

Athletic and recreation (10 activities)
From: generally informal use—exercise, games
To: greater efforts toward improvement and skilled performance

Dormitory or fraternity/sorority (10 activities)
From: general socializing
To: more personal exchanges—helping, sharing, studying together, working on projects

Experiences with faculty (10 activities)
From: routine and casual
To: more serious contacts—such as discussing careers, inviting criticisms, seeking counsel

Clubs and organizations (10 activities)
From: awareness of events and organizations
To: attending events, discussing programs, working in organizations

Experiences in writing (10 activities)
From: general concern with words, grammar, revisions
To: seeking criticism from others, greater concern with clarity and style

Personal experiences (10 activities)
From: general curiosity about understanding one's own behavior, and others—talked with friends, etc.
To: more focused and expertly informed sources of self-understanding—as in reading, taking a test, talking with a counselor

Student acquaintances (10 activities)
From: making friends with different kinds of people—breadth
To: serious conversations with people who differ from you—depth

Topics of conversation (12 items)
From: personal and interpersonal topics of immediate experience—jobs, movies, social events
To: intellectual and cultural topics concerning values and social issues

Information in conversations (6 activities)
From: conversations in which information about the topic is relatively casual and infrequently introduced
To: conversations that typically have expertise, knowledge, and persuasiveness brought to bear on the topic.

REFERENCES

The Educational Resources Information Center (ERIC) Clearinghouse on Higher Education abstracts and indexes the current literature on higher education for inclusion in ERIC's data base and announcement in ERIC's monthly bibliographic journal, *Resources in Education* (RIE). Most of these publications are available through the ERIC Document Reproduction Service (EDRS). For publications cited in this bibliography that are available from EDRS, ordering number and price code are included. Readers who wish to order a publication should write to the ERIC Document Reproduction Service, 7420 Fullerton Rd., Suite 110, Springfield, VA 22153-2852. (Phone orders with VISA or MasterCard are taken at 800-443-ERIC or 703-440-1400.) When ordering, please specify the document (ED) number. Documents are available as noted in microfiche (MF) and paper copy (PC). If you have the price code ready when you call EDRS, an exact price can be quoted. The last page of the latest issue of *Resources in Education* also has the current cost, listed by code.

Arnold, J., G. Kuh, N. Vesper, and J. Schuh. 1991. "The Influence of Student Effort, College Environment and Selected Student Characteristics on Undergraduate Student Learning and Personal Development at Metropolitan Institutions." Boston: Paper presented at the annual meeting of the Association for the Study of Higher Education. ED 339 296. 27 pp. MF–01; PC–02.

Astin, A. 1968. *The College Environment.* Washington, D.C.: American Council on Education.

———. 1973. "The Impact of Dormatory Living on Students." *Educational Record* 54: 204-10.

———. 1977. *Four Critical Years: The Effects of College on Beliefs, Attitudes, and Knowledge.* San Francisco: Jossey-Bass.

———. 1984. "Student Involvement: A Developmental Theory for Higher Education." *Journal of College Student Personnel* 25: 297-308.

———. 1985. *Achieving Educational Excellence: A Critical Assessment of Priorities and Practices in Higher Education.* San Francisco: Jossey-Bass.

———. 1993. *What Matters in College: Four Critical Years Revisited.* San Francisco: Jossey-Bass.

Baird, L. 1988. "The College Environment Revisited: A Review of Research and Theory." In *Higher Education: Handbook of Theory and Research.* Vol. 4. J. Smart, ed. New York: Agathon Press.

———. 1990. "The Undergraduate Experience: Communalities and Differences Among Colleges." *Research in Higher Education* 31(3): 271-78.

Baldwin, B. 1989. "A Primer in the Use and Interpretation of Structural Equation Models." *Measurement and Evaluation in Counseling and Development* 22: 100-12.

Bean, J. 1980. "Dropouts and Turnover: The Synthesis and Test of a Causal Model of Student Attrition." *Research in Higher Education* 12(2): 155-87.

Bean, J., and R. Bradley. 1986. "Untangling the Satisfaction-Performance Relationship for College Students." *Journal of Higher Education* 57(4): 293-412.

Bellah, R., R. Madsen, W. Sullivan, A. Swidler, and S. Tipton. 1985. *Habits of the Heart: Individualism and Commitment in American Life.* New York: Harper & Row.

Bentler, P. 1989. *EQS Structural Equations Program Manual.* Los Angeles: BMDP Statistical Software.

Bonwell, C., and J. Eison. 1991. *Active Learning: Creating Excitement in the Classroom.* ASHE-ERIC Higher Education Research Report No. 1. Washington, D.C.: Association for the Study of Higher Education. ED 336 049. 121 pp. PC–05; MF–01.

Bruffee, K. 1984. *Collaborative Learning and the 'Conversation of Mankind'* 46(7): 635-47.

Cabrera, A., M. Castaneda, A. Nora, and D. Hengstler. 1992. "The Convergence Between Two Theories of College Persistence." *Journal of Higher Education* 63(2): 143-64.

Chapman, D., and E. Pascarella. 1983. "Predictors of Academic and Social Integration of College Students." *Research in Higher Education* 19(3): 295-322.

Chickering, A.W. 1969. *Education and Identity.* San Francisco: Jossey-Bass.

Chickering, A.W., and E. Kuper. 1971. "Educational Outcomes for Commuters and Residents." *Educational Record* 52(3): 255-61.

Chickering, A.W. 1981. *The Modern American College: Responding to the New Realities of Diverse Students and a Changing Society.* San Francisco: Jossey-Bass.

Chickering, A.W., and L. Reisser. 1993. *Education and Identity.* 2d ed. San Francisco: Jossey-Bass.

Christie, N., and S. Dinham. 1991. "Institutional and External Influences on Social Integration in the Freshman Year." *Journal of Higher Education* 62(4): 412-36.

Clark, B. 1962. *Educating the Expert Society.* San Francisco: Chandler.

Copland-Wood, B. 1985. "Older Commuter Students and the Collegiate Experience: Involved or Detached?" Milwaukee: Paper presented at the conference of the American Association for Adult and Continuing Education. ED 263 398. 21 pp. MF–01; PC–01.

Crosson, P. 1988. "Four-year College and University Environments for Minority Degree Achievement." *Review of Higher Education* 11(4): 365-82.

Davis, T., and P. Murrell. 1993. "A Structural Model of Perceived Academic, Personal, and Vocational Gains Related to College Student Responsibility." *Research in Higher Education* 34(3): 267-89.

Endo, J., and R. Harpel. 1982. "The Effect of Student-Faculty Inter-action on Students' Educational Outcomes." *Research in Higher Education* 16(2): 115-38.

Fairweather, J., and D. Shaver. 1990. "A Troubled Future? Participation in Postsecondary Education by Youths with Disabilities." *Journal of Higher Education* 61(3): 332-48.

Feldman, K., and T. Newcomb. 1969. *The Impact of College on Students.* San Francisco: Jossey-Bass.

Flannelly, S. 1990. "Student Faculty Contact and Academic Quality of Effort: Excerpted Results from CSEQ Surveys, 1985-1988." University of North Carolina-Chapel Hill. ED 323 869. 7 pp. MF–01; PC–01.

Fleming, J. 1984. *Blacks in College: A Comparitive Study of Students' Success in Black and White Institutions.* San Francisco: Jossey-Bass.

Friedlander, J., P.H. Murrell, and P. McDougal. 1993. "Using the Community College Student Experiences Questionnaire to Promote Student Involvement and Achievement." In *Are We Making a Difference? Outcomes of Assessment in Higher Education.* T. Banta, ed. San Francisco: Jossey-Bass. Forthcoming.

Glover, J. 1992. "The Collegiate Experience for the 'Forgotten Majority': A Test of a Tinto Model to Explain Outcomes for Commuters in Urban Universities." Ed.D. dissertation, Memphis State University.

Hall, P., and D. Kehoe. 1971. "Student-Faculty Interaction and the Organization of the University." *Interchange* 2(4): 52-72.

Hearn, J. 1987. "Impacts of Undergraduate Experiences on Aspirations and Plans for Graduate and Professional Education." *Research in Higher Education* 27(2): 119-41.

Horowitz, H. 1987. *Campus Life: Undergraduate Cultures From the End of the Eighteenth Century to the Present.* New York: Basic Books.

Joreskog, K., and D. Sorbom. 1988. *LISREL 7: A Guide to the Program and Applications.* Chicago: SPSS.

Kuh, G., and Others. 1988. "Personal Development and the College Student Experience: A Review of the Literature." Paper prepared for the College Outcomes Evaluation Program, New Jersey Department of Higher Education. ED 304 972. 139 pp. MF–01; PC–05.

Kuh, G., and E. Whitt. 1988. *The Invisible Tapestry: Culture in American Colleges and Universities.* ASHE-ERIC Higher Education Report No. 1. Washington, D.C.: Association for the Study of Higher Education. ED 299 934. 160 pp. PC–07; MF–01.

Kuh, G., J. Schuh, E. Whitt, and Associates. 1991. *Involving Colleges.* San Francisco: Jossey-Bass.

Kuhn, T. 1970. *The Structure of Scientific Revolutions.* Chicago: University of Chicago Press.

Lenning, O., L. Munday, O. Johnson, A. Banderwell, and E. Brub. 1974. "The Many Faces of College Success and Their Nonintellective Correlates." In *Published Literatures Through the Decade of the Sixties*, Monograph No. 15. Iowa City: American College Testing.

Lickona, T. 1991. *Educating for Character: How Our Schools Can Teach Respect and Responsibility.* New York: Bantam Books.

MacGregor, J., R. Matthews, B. Smith, and F. Gabelnick. 1990. *Learning Communities: Creating Connections Among Students, Faculty and Disciplines.* New Directions for Teaching and Learning No. 41. San Francisco: Jossey-Bass.

Masland, A. 1985. "Organizational Culture in the Study of Higher Education." *The Review of Higher Education* 8(2): 157-68.

Mencke, R., C. Sahoo, and R. Kroc. 1988. "Assessing Institutional Effects on Retention." Phoenix: Paper presented at the annual meeting of the Association for Institutional Research. ED 298 855. 24 pp. MF–01; PC–01.

Moffatt, M. 1991. "College Life: Undergraduate Culture and Higher Education." *Journal of Higher Education* 62(1): 44-61.

Moos, R. 1979. *Evaluating Educational Environments.* San Francisco: Jossey-Bass.

Moran, E., and J. Volkwein. 1988. "Examining Organizational Climate in Institutions of Higher Education." *Research in Higher Education* 28(4): 367-83.

Munro, B. 1981. "Dropouts from Higher Education: Path Analysis of a National Sample." *American Educational Research Journal* 18(2): 133-41.

Murrell, P.H., and C.S. Claxton. 1987. "Experiential Learning Theory as a Guide for Effective Teaching." *Counselor Education and Supervision* 27(1): 4-14.

Murrell, P.H., and T.M. Davis. 1992. "*Assessment Strategies for Kolb's Experiential Learning Cycle.*" Unpublished paper. Memphis: Center for the Study of Higher Education, Memphis State University.

Mutter, P. 1992. "Tinto's Theory of Departure and Community College Student Persistence." *Journal of College Student Development* 33: 310-17.

Nettles, M. 1991. "Racial Similarities and Differences in the Predictors of College Student Achievement." In *College in Black and White.* W. Allen, E. Epps, and N. Haniff, eds. Albany, N.Y.: State University of New York Press.

Oliver, M. 1985. "Brown and Black in White: The Social Adjustment and Academic Performance of Chicano and Black Students in a Predominantly White University." *Urban Review* 17(1): 3-23.

Ory, J., and L. Braskamp. 1988. "Involvement and Growth of Students in Three Academic Programs." *Research in Higher Education* 28(2): 116-29.

Pace, R. 1979a. *College Student Experiences.* Los Angeles: UCLA Laboratory for Research on Higher Education.

————. 1979b. *Measuring Outcomes of College.* San Francisco: Jossey-Bass.

————. 1982. "Achievement and the Quality of Student Effort." Washington, D.C.: National Commission on Excellence in Education. ED 227 101. 40 pp. MC-01; PC–02.

————. 1984. *Measuring the Quality of College Student Experiences.* Los Angeles: UCLA Center for the Study of Evaluation. ED 255 099. 142 pp. MF–01; PC not available EDRS.

————. 1987. *CSEQ: Test Manual & Norms.* Los Angeles: UCLA Center for the Study of Evaluation.

————. 1988. "Uses of the College Student Experiences Questionnaire." St. Louis, Mo.: Paper presented at the annual meeting of the Association for the Study of Higher Education. ED 303 101. 32 pp. MF–01; PC–02.

————. 1990. *The Undergraduates: A Report of Their Activities and Progress in College in the 1980s.* Los Angeles: UCLA Center for the Study of Evaluation.

————. 1992. "Test-Retest and Other Repeated Uses of the CSEQ: Do the Results Reveal Intended Change?" Minneapolis: Paper presented at the annual meeting of the Association for the Study of Higher Education.

————. 1992. *College Student Experiences Questionnaire: Norms for the Third Edition, 1990.* Los Angeles: UCLA Center for the Study of Evaluation.

Pace, R., and G. Stern. 1958. "An Approach to the Measurement of Psychological Characteristics of College Environments." *Journal of Educational Psychology* 49: 269-77.

Palmer, P. 1983. *To Know as We are Known/A Spirituality of Education.* San Francisco: Harper & Row.

————. 1987. "Community, Conflict, and Ways of Knowing." *Change* 19(5): 20-25.

Pascarella, E. 1985. "College Environmental Influences on Learning and Cognitive Development: A Critical Review and Synthesis." In *Higher Education: Handbook of Theory and Research.* Vol. 1. J. Smart, ed. New York: Agathon Press.

————. 1991. "The Impact of College on Students: The Nature of the Evidence." *The Review of Higher Education* 14(4): 453-66.

Pascarella, E., and D. Chapman. 1983. "A Multiinstitutional, Path Analytic Validation of Tinto's Model of College Withdrawal." *American Educational Research Journal* 20(1): 87-102.

Pascarella, E., P. Duby, and B. Iverson. 1983. "A Test and Reconceptualization of a Theoretical Model of College Withdrawal in a Commuter Institution Setting." *Sociology of Education* 56: 88-100.

Pascarella, E., and P. Terenzini. 1977. "Patterns of Student-Faculty

---

Informal Relationships and Freshman Year Educational Outcomes."
Journal of Higher Education 48: 540-52.

———. 1980. "Predicting Freshman Persistence and Voluntary Drop-
out Decisions from a Theoretical Model." *Journal of Higher Education* 51(1): 60-75.

———. 1983. "Predicting Voluntary Freshman Year Persistence/With-
drawal Behavior in a Residential University: A Path Analytic Validation of Tinto's Model." *Journal of Educational Psychology* 75:
215-26.

———. 1991. *How College Affects Students.* San Francisco: Jossey-
Bass.

Rootman, I. 1972. "Voluntary Withdrawal from a Total Adult Socializing Organization: A Model." *Sociology of Education* 45: 258-70.

Scherer, M., M. Stinson, and G. Walter. 1987. "Factors Affecting Persistence of Deaf College Students." Washington, D.C.: Paper presented at the annual meeting of the American Educational Research
Association. ED 291 187. 35 pp. MF–01; PC–02.

Smith, V., and A. Bernstein. 1979. *The Impersonal Campus: Options
for Reorganizing Colleges to Increase Student Involvement, Learning and Development.* San Francisco: Jossey-Bass.

Spady, W. 1970. "Dropouts from Higher Education: An Interdisci-
plinary Review and Synthesis." *Interchange* 1(1): 64-85.

———. 1971. "Dropouts from Higher Education: Toward an Empirical Model." *Interchange* 2(3): 38-62.

Stone, J., and C. Strange. 1989. "Quality of Student Experiences of
Freshman Intercollegiate Athletes." *Journal of College Student
Development* 30: 148-53.

Stage, F. 1987. "Outcomes and Development: Separate Notions or
Parts of One Whole." Baltimore: Paper presented at the annual
meeting of the Association for the Study of Higher Education.
ED 292 402. 21 pp. MF–01; PC–01.

———. 1989. "An Alternative to Path Analysis: A Demonstration of
LISREL Using Students' Commitment to an Institution." *Journal
of College Student Development* 30: 129-35.

Stern, G. 1970. *People in Context: Measuring Person-Environment
Congruence in Education and Industry.* New York: John Wiley.

Stoecker, J., E. Pascarella, and L. Wolfle. 1988. "Persistence in Higher
Education: A Nine-Year Test of a Theoretical Model." *Journal of
College Student Development* 29: 196-209.

Suen, H. 1983. "Alienation and Attrition of Black College Students
on a Predominantly White Campus." *Journal of College Student
Personnel* 24: 117-21.

Task Group on General Education. 1988. *A New Vitality in General
Education. Planning, Teaching, and Supporting Effective Liberal
Learning.* Washington, D.C.: Association of American Colleges.
ED 290 387. 64 pp. MF–01; PC not available EDRS.

Terenzini, P. 1987. "A Review of Selected Theoretical Models of Student Development and Collegiate Impact." Baltimore: Paper presented at the annual meeting of the Association for the Study of Higher Education. ED 292 382. 39 pp. MF–01; PC–02.

Terenzini, P., and E. Pascarella. 1977. "Voluntary Freshman Attrition and Patterns of Social and Academic Integration in a University: A Test of a Conceptual Model." *Research in Higher Education* 6: 25-43.

———. 1980. "Student/Faculty Relationships and Freshman Year Educational Outcomes: A Further Investigation." *Journal of College Student Personnel* 21: 521-28.

———. 1990. "Twenty Years of Research on College Students: Lessons for Future Research." Louisville, Ky.: Paper presented at the annual meeting of the Association for Institutional Research. ED 321 697. 18 pp. MF–01; PC–01.

Terenzini, P., C. Theophilides, and W. Lorang. 1984. "Influences on Students' Perceptions of Their Academic Skill Development During College." *Journal of Higher Education* 55(5): 621-36.

Terenzini, P., and T. Wright. 1987. "Influences on Students' Academic Growth During Four Years of College." *Research in Higher Education* 26(2): 161-79.

Tinto, V. 1975. "Droupout from Higher Education: A Theoretical Synthesis of Recent Research." *Review of Educational Research* 45: 89-125.

———. 1987. *Leaving College: Rethinking the Causes and Cures of Student Attrition.* Chicago: University of Chicago Press.

Volkwein, J., M. King, and P. Terenzini. 1986. "Student-Faculty Relationships and Intellectual Growth Among Transfer Students." *Journal of Higher Education* 57(4): 413-30.

Walleri, R., and M. Peglow-Hoch. 1988. "Case Studies of Non-Traditional High Risk Students: Does Social and Academic Integration Apply?" Phoenix: Paper presented at the annual meeting of the Association for Institutional Research. ED 298 863. 22 pp. MF–01; PC–01.

Walter, G., and J. DeCaro. 1986. "Attrition Among Hearing-Impaired College Students in the U.S." Washington, D.C.: National Technical Institute for the Deaf. ED 296 521. 13 pp. MF–01; PC–01.

Walter, G., and W. Welsh. 1986. "Providing for the Needs of Handicapped Students in a Postsecondary Environment." Washington, D.C.: National Technical Institute for the Deaf. ED 296 517. 10 pp. MF–01; PC–01.

Weidman, J. 1985. "Retention of Nontraditional Students in Postsecondary Education." Chicago: Paper presented at the annual meeting of the American Educational Research Association. ED 261 195. 16 pp. MF–01; PC–01.

Widick, C., C. Parker, and L. Knefelkamp. 1978. "Erick Erickson and

Psychosocial Development." In *Applying New Developmental Findings*. L. Knefelkamp, C. Widick, and C. Parker, eds. New Directions in Student Services. San Francisco: Jossey-Bass.

INDEX

commuter
        campus commitment influenced by academic integration,
            47
        experience, 42-43
commuting effect on student degree completion, 60
conditional effects of college, 13
content domains. See scales
Cooperative Institutional Research Program, 18, 30, 32, 40, 43,
    58, 62
Cooperative Learning: Increasing College Faculty Instructional
    Productivity, xv
cooperative learning, 73
course learning scale, 81
covariance structure analysis approaches, 26
Critical Thinking: Theory, Research, Practice, and Possibilities, xv
Crosson (1988), 33
CSEQ. See College Student Experience Questionnaire
"culture of dependency," 2

D
Davis and Murrell (1993), 50, 62, 63
Davis, Jane Furr, xvii
deaf students, social integration key variable in retention of, 35
Dickens, Charles, 1
Didion, Joan, 27
Dormitory or fraternity/sorority, effort scale, 81

E
effort scales, 81-82
Emerson, Ralph Waldo, 11
Endo and Harple (1982), 55
environmental press, 20
epistemology, 4
Experiences in writing, effort scale, 82
Experiences with faculty, effort scale, 82
Experiential Learning Model, 73

F
facilities use by students, measurement of, 6
facilities related to the arts, effort scale, 81
faculty
        contact key in persistence, 57
        discussion on intellectual development, 55
Fairweather and Shaver (1990), 34
Feldman and Newcomb (1969), 14
Fielding, H., 37
"fit," concept of, 46-47
Flannelly (1990), 61

Fleming (1984), 33

G

General causal Model, 38
Gide, Andre, 17
Glover (1992), 44, 47, 57
"God resides in the details," 21

H

Habits of the Heart. See Bellah, Robert
Hall and Kehoe (1971), 39, 44
Hearn, James (1987), 32, 56
Helme, 53
high school grades, significant background variable, 31
How College Affects Students. See Pascarella and Terenzini (1991)
human aggregate, of college environment, 37

I

Information in conversations, effort scale, 82
input process-output model for analysis of college effects, 18
Input-Environment-Outcomes model, 30, 59
institution fully committed to student involvement, definition of,
    78
Institutional types, 41
institutional indifference toward student behavior, rise of, 79
integrative theory, institutions lack of, 17
interviews analysis, 56, 57
investment of effort in student personal and social relationships,
    6-7
Involvement in Learning report, 71, 72
involvement, key to developing student talent, 66
"Involving Colleges" study, 50

J

job holding effect on degree completion, 60

K

Kingery, Dwane, xvii
Kolb, David, 73
Kuh et al. (1991), 50, 62
Kuhn, Thomas, 17

L

Learning process
        from lecture, students record in way can relate to other data,
        xv
        dependent on students taking responsibility for using, xv
        college and teacher responsibility, 6

Q

"quality of effort," 11-12
> frequency and consistency of effort crucially important, 11
> scales, 6
quality student-faculty contact on academic content, 56

R

rating scales, 49
Regression analysis, 55-57
> and discriminant analysis, 54
residential four-year school,
> commitment influenced by social integration, 47
responsibility of colleges to clearly articulate their mission, 13
responsibility, dialogue between students and faculty on areas of, 76-77
retention research and college outcomes, focus and direction for, 19, 31
Rockefeller, John D. Jr., 1
Rootman (1972), 47

S

SAT and faculty discussion on academic performance, 55
satisfactory college outcomes, requires student integration, 66
Scherer, Stinson, and Walter (1987), 34-35
Schwartz, Delmore, 69
SES. See socioeconomic status
sex-by-race causal models, 32
socioeconomic status, 30, 31, 56
Smith and Bernstein (1979). See also The Impersonal Campus
social climate, 13
social integration. See also persistence and academic integration
> distinction from academic integration, 53
> importance in study of student retention, 18
> important in minority persistence, 56
> key for residential, 56
> minimal influence on persistence, 57
> role, 58
Spady (1970, 1971), 18
Stage (1989), 26
State University of New York at Albany, 29
Stern, George, 12
Stoecker, Pascarella, and Wolfle (1988), 32, 56
Stone and Strange (1989), 62
structural modeling. See path analysis
Student acquaintances, effort scale, 82
student athletes, 62
student background in shaping college outcomes, role of, 21
student behavior, at center of academic enterprise, 20

University of California at Los Angeles, 33, 34
       Center for the Study of Evaluation, 62
University of North Carolina, 61

V

vocational and career gains importance, 14
Volkwein, King and Terenzini (1986), 29, 56

W

Walleri and Peglow Hoch (1988), 57
Walter and DeCaro (1986), 34
Weidman (1985), 56
What Matters in College. See Astin (1993)
Williford, Lucy, xvii
women. student retention models, 31

ASHE-ERIC HIGHER EDUCATION REPORTS

Since 1983, the Association for the Study of Higher Education (ASHE) and the Educational Resources Information Center (ERIC) Clearinghouse on Higher Education, a sponsored project of the School of Education and Human Development at The George Washington University, have cosponsored the *ASHE-ERIC Higher Education Report* series. The 1993 series is the twenty-second overall and the fifth to be published by the School of Education and Human Development at the George Washington University.

Each monograph is the definitive analysis of a tough higher education problem, based on thorough research of pertinent literature and institutional experiences. Topics are identified by a national survey. Noted practitioners and scholars are then commissioned to write the reports, with experts providing critical reviews of each manuscript before publication.

Eight monographs (10 before 1985) in the ASHE-ERIC Higher Education Report series are published each year and are available on individual and subscription bases. Subscription to eight issues is $98.00 annually; $78 to members of AAHE, AIR, or AERA; and $68 to ASHE members. All foreign subscribers must include an additional $10 per series year for postage.

To order, use the order form on the last page of this book. Regular prices are as follows:

Series	Price
1993	$18.00
1988 to 92	$17.00
before 1988	$15.00

Discounts on non-subscription orders:
• Bookstores, and current members of AERA, AIR, AAHE and ASHE, receive a 25% discount.
• Bulk: For non-bookstore, non-member orders of 10 or more books, deduct 10%.

Shipping costs are as follows:
• U.S. address: 5% of invoice subtotal for orders over $50.00; $2.50 for each order with an invoice subtotal of $50.00 or less.
• Foreign: $2.50 per book.

All orders under $45.00 must be prepaid. Make check payable to ASHE-ERIC. For Visa or MasterCard, include card number, expiration date and signature.

Address order to
ASHE-ERIC Higher Education Reports
The George Washington University
1 Dupont Circle, Suite 630
Washington, DC 20036
Or phone (202) 296-2597, toll-free: 800-773-ERIC.
Write or call for a complete catalog.

1993 ASHE-ERIC Higher Education Reports

1. The Department Chair: New Roles, Responsibilities and Challenges
   Alan T. Seagren, John W. Creswell, and Daniel W. Wheeler

2. Sexual Harassment in Higher Education: From Conflict to Community
   Robert O. Riggs, Patricia H. Murrell, and JoAnn C. Cutting

3. Chicanos in Higher Education: Issues and Dilemmas for the 21st Century
   by Adalberto Aguirre, Jr., and Ruben O. Martinez

4. Academic Freedom in American Higher Education: Rights, Responsibilities, and Limitations
   by Robert K. Poch

5. Making Sense of the Dollars: The Costs and Uses of Faculty Compensation
   by Kathryn M. Moore and Marilyn J. Amey

6. Enhancing Promotion, Tenure and Beyond: Faculty Socialization as Cultural Process
   by William G. Tierney and Robert A. Rhoads

7. New Perspectives for Student Affairs Professionals: Evolving Realities, Responsibilities and Roles
   by Peter H. Garland and Thomas W. Grace

1992 ASHE-ERIC Higher Education Reports

1. The Leadership Compass: Values and Ethics in Higher Education
   John R. Wilcox and Susan L. Ebbs

2. Preparing for a Global Community: Achieving an International Perspective in Higher Education
   Sarah M. Pickert

3. Quality: Transforming Postsecondary Education
   Ellen Earle Chaffee and Lawrence A. Sherr

4. Faculty Job Satisfaction: Women and Minorities in Peril
   Martha Wingard Tack and Carol Logan Patitu

5. Reconciling Rights and Responsibilities of Colleges and Students: Offensive Speech, Assembly, Drug Testing, and Safety
   Annette Gibbs

6. Creating Distinctiveness: Lessons from Uncommon Colleges and Universities
   Barbara K. Townsend, L. Jackson Newell, and Michael D. Wiese

7. Instituting Enduring Innovations: Achieving Continuity of Change in Higher Education
   Barbara K. Curry

8. Crossing Pedagogical Oceans: International Teaching Assistants in U.S. Undergraduate Education
   Rosslyn M. Smith, Patricia Byrd, Gayle L. Nelson, Ralph Pat Barrett, and Janet C. Constantinides

1991 ASHE-ERIC Higher Education Reports

1. Active Learning: Creating Excitement in the Classroom
   Charles C. Bonwell and James A. Eison

2. Realizing Gender Equality in Higher Education: The Need to Integrate Work/Family Issues
   Nancy Hensel

3. Academic Advising for Student Success: A System of Shared Responsibility
   Susan H. Frost

4. Cooperative Learning: Increasing College Faculty Instructional Productivity
   David W. Johnson, Roger T. Johnson, and Karl A. Smith

5. High School–College Partnerships: Conceptual Models, Programs, and Issues
   Arthur Richard Greenberg

6. Meeting the Mandate: Renewing the College and Departmental Curriculum
   William Toombs and William Tierney

7. Faculty Collaboration: Enhancing the Quality of Scholarship and Teaching
   Ann E. Austin and Roger G. Baldwin

8. Strategies and Consequences: Managing the Costs in Higher Education
   John S. Waggaman

1990 ASHE-ERIC Higher Education Reports

1. The Campus Green: Fund Raising in Higher Education
   Barbara E. Brittingham and Thomas R. Pezzullo

2. The Emeritus Professor: Old Rank - New Meaning
   James E. Mauch, Jack W. Birch, and Jack Matthews

3. "High Risk" Students in Higher Education: Future Trends
   Dionne J. Jones and Betty Collier Watson

4. Budgeting for Higher Education at the State Level: Enigma, Paradox, and Ritual
   Daniel T. Layzell and Jan W. Lyddon

5. Proprietary Schools: Programs, Policies, and Prospects
   John B. Lee and Jamie P. Merisotis

6. College Choice: Understanding Student Enrollment Behavior
   Michael B. Paulsen

7. Pursuing Diversity: Recruiting College Minority Students
   Barbara Astone and Elsa Nuñez-Wormack

8. Social Consciousness and Career Awareness: Emerging Link
   in Higher Education
   John S. Swift, Jr.

1989 ASHE-ERIC Higher Education Reports

1. Making Sense of Administrative Leadership: The 'L' Word in
   Higher Education
   Estela M. Bensimon, Anna Neumann, and Robert Birnbaum

2. Affirmative Rhetoric, Negative Action: African-American and
   Hispanic Faculty at Predominantly White Universities
   Valora Washington and William Harvey

3. Postsecondary Developmental Programs: A Traditional Agenda
   with New Imperatives
   Louise M. Tomlinson

4. The Old College Try: Balancing Athletics and Academics in
   Higher Education
   John R. Thelin and Lawrence L. Wiseman

5. The Challenge of Diversity: Involvement or Alienation in the
   Academy?
   Daryl G. Smith

6. Student Goals for College and Courses: A Missing Link in Assessing and Improving Academic Achievement
   Joan S. Stark, Kathleen M. Shaw, and Malcolm A. Lowther

7. The Student as Commuter: Developing a Comprehensive Institutional Response
   Barbara Jacoby

8. Renewing Civic Capacity: Preparing College Students for Service
   and Citizenship
   Suzanne W. Morse

1988 ASHE-ERIC Higher Education Reports

1. The Invisible Tapestry: Culture in American Colleges and
   Universities
   George D. Kuh and Elizabeth J. Whitt

2. Critical Thinking: Theory, Research, Practice, and Possibilities
   Joanne Gainen Kurfiss

3. Developing Academic Programs: The Climate for Innovation
   Daniel T. Seymour

4. Peer Teaching: To Teach is To Learn Twice
   Neal A. Whitman

5. Higher Education and State Governments: Renewed Partnership,
   Cooperation, or Competition?
   Edward R. Hines

6. Entrepreneurship and Higher Education: Lessons for Colleges,
   Universities, and Industry
   James S. Fairweather

7. Planning for Microcomputers in Higher Education: Strategies
   for the Next Generation
   *Reynolds Ferrante, John Hayman, Mary Susan Carlson, and
   Harry Phillips*

8. The Challenge for Research in Higher Education: Harmonizing
   Excellence and Utility
   Alan W. Lindsay and Ruth T. Neumann

1987 ASHE-ERIC Higher Education Reports

1. Incentive Early Retirement Programs for Faculty: Innovative
   Responses to a Changing Environment
   Jay L. Chronister and Thomas R. Kepple, Jr.

2. Working Effectively with Trustees: Building Cooperative Campus
   Leadership
   Barbara E. Taylor

3. Formal Recognition of Employer-Sponsored Instruction: Conflict
   and Collegiality in Postsecondary Education
   Nancy S. Nash and Elizabeth M. Hawthorne

4. Learning Styles: Implications for Improving Educational Practices
   Charles S. Claxton and Patricia H. Murrell

5. Higher Education Leadership: Enhancing Skills through Professional Development Programs
   Sharon A. McDade

6. Higher Education and the Public Trust: Improving Stature in
   Colleges and Universities
   Richard L. Alfred and Julie Weissman

7. College Student Outcomes Assessment: A Talent Development
   Perspective
   Maryann Jacobi, Alexander Astin, and Frank Ayala, Jr.

8. Opportunity from Strength: Strategic Planning Clarified with
   Case Examples
   Robert G. Cope

1986 ASHE-ERIC Higher Education Reports

1. Post-tenure Faculty Evaluation: Threat or Opportunity?
   Christine M. Licata

2. Blue Ribbon Commissions and Higher Education: Changing Academe from the Outside
   Janet R. Johnson and Laurence R. Marcus

3. Responsive Professional Education: Balancing Outcomes and Opportunities
   Joan S. Stark, Malcolm A. Lowther, and Bonnie M.K. Hagerty

4. Increasing Students' Learning: A Faculty Guide to Reducing Stress among Students
   Neal A. Whitman, David C. Spendlove, and Claire H. Clark

5. Student Financial Aid and Women: Equity Dilemma?
   Mary Moran

6. The Master's Degree: Tradition, Diversity, Innovation
   Judith S. Glazer

7. The College, the Constitution, and the Consumer Student: Implications for Policy and Practice
   Robert M. Hendrickson and Annette Gibbs

8. Selecting College and University Personnel: The Quest and the Question
   Richard A. Kaplowitz

*Out-of-print. Available through EDRS. Call 1-800-443-ERIC.

Quantity **Amount**

_____ Please begin my subscription to the 1993 *ASHE-ERIC Higher Education Reports* at $98.00, 32% off the cover price, starting with Report 1, 1993. _____

_____ Please send a complete set of the 1992 *ASHE-ERIC Higher Education Reports* at $90.00, 33% off the cover price. _____

_____ Outside the U.S., add $10.00 per series for postage. _____

SHIPPING: **U.S. Orders:** *For subtotal (before discount) of $50.00 or less, add $2.50. For subtotal over $50.00, add 5% of subtotal. Call for rush service options.* **Foreign Orders:** *$2.50 per book.* **U.S. Subscriptions:** *Included in price.* **Foreign Subscriptions:** *Add $10.00.*

PLEASE SEND ME THE FOLLOWING REPORTS:

Quantity	Report No.	Year	Title	Amount

Subtotal:	
Shipping:	
Total Due:	

Please check one of the following:
☐ Check enclosed, payable to GWU–ERIC.
☐ Purchase order attached ($45.00 minimum).
☐ Charge my credit card indicated below:
  ☐ Visa ☐ MasterCard

Expiration Date _____

Name _____

Title _____

Institution _____

Address _____

City _____ State _____ Zip _____

Phone _____ Fax _____ Telex _____

Signature _____ Date _____

SEND ALL ORDERS TO:
ASHE-ERIC Higher Education Reports
The George Washington University
One Dupont Circle, Suite 630
Washington, DC 20036-1183
Phone: (202) 296-2597
Toll-free: 800-773-ERIC

ORDER FORM 93-8

Quantity **Amount**

_____ Please begin my subscription to the 1993 *ASHE-ERIC Higher Education Reports* at $98.00, 32% off the cover price, starting with Report 1, 1993. _____

_____ Please send a complete set of the 1992 *ASHE-ERIC Higher Education Reports* at $90.00, 33% off the cover price. _____

_____ Outside the U.S., add $10.00 per series for postage. _____

SHIPPING: **U.S. Orders:** *For subtotal (before discount) of $50.00 or less, add $2.50. For subtotal over $50.00, add 5% of subtotal. Call for rush service options.* **Foreign Orders:** *$2.50 per book.* **U.S. Subscriptions:** *Included in price.* **Foreign Subscriptions:** *Add $10.00.*

PLEASE SEND ME THE FOLLOWING REPORTS:

Quantity	Report No.	Year	Title	Amount

Please check one of the following: **Subtotal:** _____
☐ Check enclosed, payable to GWU–ERIC.   **Shipping:** _____
☐ Purchase order attached ($45.00 minimum).   **Total Due:** _____
☐ Charge my credit card indicated below:
     ☐ Visa   ☐ MasterCard

Expiration Date _____

Name _____

Title _____

Institution _____

Address _____

City _____ State _____ Zip _____

Phone _____ Fax _____ Telex _____

Signature _____ Date _____

SEND ALL ORDERS TO:
ASHE-ERIC Higher Education Reports
The George Washington University
One Dupont Circle, Suite 630
Washington, DC 20036-1183
Phone: (202) 296-2597
Toll-free: 800-773-ERIC